The Moral Injury Handbook

The Moral Injury Handbook

Theory, Care, and Repair in Public and Faith Contexts: A Practical Guide for Clergy, Disaster Responders, and Public Leaders

G. C. SMITH

RESOURCE *Publications* · Eugene, Oregon

THE MORAL INJURY HANDBOOK
Theory, Care, and Repair in Public and Faith Contexts: A Practical Guide for Clergy, Disaster Responders, and Public Leaders

Resource Publications
An Imprint of Wipf and Stock Publishers
199 W. 8th Ave., Suite 3
Eugene, OR 97401

www.wipfandstock.com

PAPERBACK ISBN: 979-8-3852-8512-9
HARDCOVER ISBN: 979-8-3852-8513-6
EBOOK ISBN: 979-8-3852-8514-3

VERSION NUMBER 07/16/26

The views expressed in this book are those of the author and do not necessarily reflect the official policies or positions of the American Red Cross, Presbyterian Disaster Assistance, or any other organization with which the author has served or been affiliated. Stories and examples have been anonymized or adapted to protect the privacy of individuals and communities.

This book is intended for educational, pastoral, and professional development purposes. It is not intended as a substitute for professional medical, psychological, psychiatric, legal, or other clinical advice.

For those who carry what does not resolve—

who continue when there is no clear ending,
who remain when explanation is not enough,
who live with what stays.

This book is for you.

Contents

Introduction

Naming What Remains

He can still see the room.

Nothing about it stands out at first. A table. A chair. A decision that needed to be made within the time that was given. There were reasons. There was pressure. There were constraints that made the outcome seem necessary.

And it was.

At the time, there was no clear alternative. The decision was made, the moment passed, and the work continued.

No one stopped.

No one said anything was wrong.

But later—sometimes much later—something began to return.

Not as a memory alone, but as a question that did not settle. Not as doubt about what was done, but as a sense that something within it remained unfinished.

He can explain the decision.

He cannot dismiss what remains.

—

She remembers standing just outside the doorway.

She was not the one making the decision. She was not the one with authority. What was happening in the room was not hers to determine.

But she could see it.

She understood enough to know what it would mean. She felt the weight of it as it unfolded, even as she remained where she was—present, aware, and unable to change what was happening.

Later, when it was over, there was nothing to point to.
She had done what she was allowed to do.
She had stayed within her role.
No one asked anything more of her.
But something stayed with her.
Not because she had acted,
but because she had been there.
She can describe what happened.
She cannot set down what remains.

—

These are not rare experiences.

—

There are experiences that do not end when they are over.

The moment passes. The decision is made. The event concludes. And yet something continues. It returns without invitation, lingers without resolution, and resists explanation.

It remains.

This book begins there—not with what can be solved, but with what does not settle.

Moral injury is often described as the result of a difficult or troubling experience, but that description is not sufficient. Many difficult experiences pass. Many troubling moments are absorbed into memory and begin to recede.

Moral injury does not.

It persists because it is not only about what happened.

It is about what it means.

And what it means does not remain contained within the moment in which it occurred. It extends, shaping how we understand ourselves, how we understand others, and how we understand the world we inhabit.

This is what distinguishes moral injury from other forms of distress. It is not only emotional.

It is moral.

It reaches into the frameworks by which we interpret action, responsibility, consequence, and identity. Those frameworks do not simply disappear.

They are carried.

THE STRUCTURE BENEATH THE EXPERIENCE

When something remains, it is not random.

It is structured.

Even when it feels disordered, there is an underlying pattern to how the experience is held and interpreted. In this book, that structure is named through a framework:

M.O.R.A.L.

Not as a formula to be applied, but as a way of seeing what is already present.

M—MEANING

Every moral experience carries meaning—sometimes immediately, sometimes over time. Meaning is not fixed. It shifts as we reflect, revisit, and continue.

What once felt necessary may come to feel costly. What once felt justified may come to feel unresolved.

Meaning is not what happened.

It is how what happened is understood.

And that understanding continues to unfold.

O—OBLIGATION

Moral injury is closely tied to responsibility—not only what we did, but what we believe we should have done; not only what was required, but what was expected by ourselves, by others, and by the roles we inhabit.

Obligation rarely ends with the moment.

It continues—sometimes clearly defined, sometimes open-ended, sometimes impossible to fulfill.

R—RELATIONSHIP

Moral experience is never isolated. It is always connected—to others, to systems, to communities, to institutions.

When something does not settle, those relationships shift. Trust may change. Distance may emerge. Connection may feel altered.

The experience is not only carried internally.

It is carried relationally.

A—ACTION

Moral injury is rooted in action—something done, not done, witnessed, or allowed.

Action creates consequence, and consequence does not end when the action is over. It continues in memory, in effect, and in meaning.

L—LEGACY

What remains does not stay in the past.

It becomes part of what continues, shaping how we move forward, how we decide, how we respond, and how we understand ourselves.

Legacy is not what was intended.

It is what endures.

NOT A PROBLEM TO SOLVE

Much of what we are taught about difficulty assumes resolution—that with enough understanding, enough time, enough reflection, what troubles us will eventually settle.

Sometimes that is true.

But not always.

Moral injury does not follow that pattern. It does not resolve because it has been understood, disappear because it has been named, or conclude because time has passed.

It remains.

And when it remains, the question changes—not How do I get past this? but How do I live with this?

This is the shift that shapes this book: from resolution to integration, from ending to continuation.

WHAT THIS BOOK OFFERS

This book does not offer a way to remove what remains.

It offers a way to:

- Recognize what is present
- Understand how it has taken shape
- Remain with it without being overtaken
- Integrate it into a life that continues

It moves through four primary movements—foundations, pathways, contexts, and response—each building toward a way of living with what does not resolve.

Throughout, the focus remains consistent:

Not on resolving what cannot be resolved,
but on learning how to carry it.

WHO THIS BOOK IS FOR

This book is written for those who carry something that has not settled—for those who have made decisions that continue, who have witnessed what they cannot forget, and who live with responsibility that does not end when the moment passes.

It is also written for those who remain with others:

- Clergy
- Disaster responders
- Caregivers
- Leaders
- Anyone who sits with what does not resolve

You will not find simple answers here.

But you will find language, structure, and practices that allow you to continue.

A WAY OF READING

This book is not meant to be rushed. There will be places where you recognize something immediately, places where meaning shifts only over time, and places where what is written may not yet feel accessible.

This is part of the work.

You do not need to resolve what you encounter here.

You need only to notice it, name it, and allow it to be present.

BEGINNING

If something remains with you, you are already within this work.

You do not need to arrive anywhere else.

You do not need to complete it.

You begin by recognizing what is already there—
and by continuing.

REFLECTION

- What, if anything, remains with you as you finish this introduction?
- Where do you notice something in your own experience that has not settled?
- What would it mean, for now, not to resolve it—but simply to recognize it?

SECTION I

Foundations of Moral Injury

Chapter 1

What Is Moral Injury?

PART 1—THE MOMENT THAT DOES NOT RESOLVE

IT DID NOT SEEM like a defining moment at the time.

There was no announcement, no clear boundary around it, no internal signal that said this one will matter more than the others. It arrived the way many consequential moments arrive—quietly, embedded within the ordinary movement of responsibility. One decision among many. One response made in the midst of urgency. One turn taken while other turns remained possible only in theory.

There were too many needs and not enough time. There always are.

He moved as he had been trained to move. Assessment first. Prioritization next. Action after that. The sequence was familiar enough that it no longer felt like a sequence. It felt like instinct. He knew how to sort the field quickly, how to identify immediate need, how to narrow attention without becoming immobilized by the full weight of what stood before him. This is what experience does. It turns effort into rhythm. It gives motion a kind of confidence.

There was steadiness in that rhythm, even when the situation itself was anything but steady. You rely on what you know. You trust the process. You move.

And yet, within that movement, there was a moment.

It was not long. It was not dramatic. No one around him would have noticed it. It did not interrupt the pace of the work or announce itself as morally significant. But it existed. However briefly, he became aware that more than one thing was being asked of him and that he could not fully answer all of it.

Two needs stood before him. Both real. Both urgent. Both deserving attention. There was no obvious hierarchy that made the decision clean, no single piece of information that relieved him of responsibility. Both carried weight. Both mattered. And both could not be met in the same way at the same time.

He chose.

He had to.

The choice was made quickly, almost automatically—guided by training, shaped by experience, constrained by the limits of time, resources, and what he could see in the moment. Then he moved on, because that is what the work requires. You do not linger. You do not dwell. You do not stand in the middle of action and perform an ethical seminar for yourself. You decide, and then you go to the next need, the next responsibility, the next demand.

The system depends on that movement. Other people depend on it.

For a while, the moment seemed complete.

Later, when the urgency had passed and the movement had slowed, the moment returned—not fully, not as a complete replay, but in fragments. A partial image. A bodily memory of turning. The sense of one direction taken and another left behind. The experience came back in pieces rather than in sequence, as though the mind itself had not yet decided what, exactly, needed to be held onto.

At first, he treated it the way he treated other difficult decisions. He acknowledged it privately and assumed it would pass. Part of the work. Part of the cost. Part of what it means to function in situations where clarity is rarely complete and timing is never ideal.

But it did not pass.

It stayed.

Not loudly. Not in a way that disrupted his external functioning. He kept working. He showed up the next day. He made other decisions, responded to other people, completed other tasks. The structure of his life remained outwardly intact. From the outside, nothing had changed.

From the inside, something had shifted.

It was subtle at first. Almost imperceptible. A question emerged quietly, without force:

Was that the right choice?

He answered it the way he had been trained to answer. Yes. It followed protocol. It aligned with what was required. It was the best available decision under the conditions he faced.

That should have settled it.

But it didn't.

The question returned.

Not louder.

Not more dramatic.

Just more persistent.

Was it right?

He began to notice that the answer he could give did not fully quiet what he was feeling. There was a gap between explanation and resolution, between what he could justify and what he could settle. He could explain the decision to someone else. He could defend it. He could place it within the accepted logic of the situation.

But he could not quiet it within himself.

This is often how such moments begin to reveal themselves—not as crises, not as obvious breakdowns, but as experiences that refuse to resolve. They do not interrupt the day in the way acute emergencies do. They do not demand attention with the force of panic. Instead, they wait. They return in stillness—in the drive home, in the pause between tasks, in the strange, quiet minute before sleep.

They do not ask to be solved.

They ask to be understood.

And that is precisely what makes them difficult. The moment has already passed. The decision cannot be undone. There is no alternate version of events available for comparison. No corrective action can be taken against the fact that the choice has already been made.

And yet something remains unfinished.

He found himself returning to the same sequence again and again—not reliving it as danger, but revisiting it as meaning.

Why that choice?

What did I miss?

Was there something else I could have done?

The questions did not accuse him directly. They did not become theatrical. They did not spiral into catastrophe. They simply remained.

And in remaining, they began to reveal something deeper than the moment itself.

What troubled him was not only what happened. It was what the event had begun to mean.

PART 2—NAMING WHAT DOES NOT SETTLE

At some point, the question changes.

It is no longer simply, Why does this stay with me? It becomes, What is this?

That shift matters. Without language, experience remains diffuse. It is felt but not clearly understood, carried but not well defined. A person may know that something is wrong without being able to say what kind of wrongness it is. They may recognize that a moment continues to weigh on them without knowing how to interpret that weight. What cannot be named is difficult to engage, and what is difficult to engage is often either minimized or carried in silence.

This is where the concept of moral injury becomes necessary—not as a fashionable phrase, and not as a label imposed from outside the experience, but as a recognition of something already taking place.

Moral injury refers to the distress that arises when a person encounters a situation that violates, burdens, confuses, or exceeds their moral framework. It involves experiences in which one participates in, witnesses, or cannot prevent something that conflicts with one's understanding of what is right. It may involve action. It may involve inaction. It may involve complicity, helplessness, betrayal, or some mixture of all four. What matters is not simply that something difficult happened. What matters is that what happened has become morally significant in a way that remains unresolved.

That last phrase is important.

Moral injury is not defined primarily by the event itself. It is defined by the meaning of the event.

Two people may encounter the same circumstances, make similar decisions, and emerge carrying the experience in different ways. One may integrate the moment into an existing understanding of responsibility and move forward. The other may continue to return to the moment, not because memory is malfunctioning, but because meaning has not settled.

The difference is not only in what happened.

It is in how what happened is understood.

This is why moral injury lingers. It is not simply remembered. It remains unresolved.

It is also why moral injury is often confused with other forms of distress. On the surface, it can resemble trauma, burnout, grief, regret, or exhaustion. Elements of those experiences may certainly be present. But the central disturbance in moral injury is different.

Trauma is rooted in threat. Its central question is, Am I safe? Trauma concerns danger, vulnerability, exposure, and the body's response to overwhelming conditions.

Burnout is rooted in depletion. Its central question is, Do I have anything left? Burnout concerns overextension, exhaustion, emotional wear, and the erosion of sustainable capacity.

Moral injury is rooted in violation, burden, or rupture at the level of meaning. Its central question is, Was this right?

That distinction matters because each of these experiences points toward different kinds of care. Safety does not resolve a question of moral meaning. Rest does not resolve a question of right and wrong. A person may be safe and still morally unsettled. They may sleep and still wake with the same unresolved question.

Moral injury requires engagement with meaning.

This is why the mind often first moves toward explanation. After a morally difficult event, the individual begins by stabilizing the experience with phrases that preserve coherence: I did what I was supposed to do. There was no other option. Anyone in my position would have done the same. These explanations are often true. They are not trivial. They may be necessary. They allow a person to continue without immediately collapsing under the weight of what has happened.

But over time, they may begin to show their limits.

Not because they are incorrect.

Because they are incomplete.

They explain the logic of the decision. They do not resolve its meaning.

And moral injury resides precisely there—in the unresolved relationship between action and meaning.

As interpretation deepens, the questions change. They move beyond procedure and into identity.

What does this say about me?

What kind of person makes that choice?

What does it mean that I was part of that?

These are not merely cognitive questions. They are moral questions. They signal that the event is no longer being processed as a discrete piece of experience. It is being placed within a deeper framework of meaning—a framework involving what matters, what is expected, what counts as right, what one is responsible for, and who one understands oneself to be.

When that framework holds, difficult events may still hurt, but they remain intelligible. When that framework begins to destabilize, the event becomes harder to carry.

What once felt clear now feels uncertain.

What once felt settled now feels unresolved.

This is not the total loss of meaning. It is the weakening of the structure that once held meaning together.

That weakening may be gradual. It may not announce itself. A person may continue to function well while internally losing confidence in how to understand what has happened. They may still perform their role competently. They may still make sound decisions. They may still appear strong, clear, and dependable.

And yet, internally, something has changed.

They can explain the event.

They cannot fully reconcile it.

This is why moral injury so often goes unrecognized. It can exist beneath competence, alongside effectiveness, within continued performance. It does not always appear as visible crisis. Sometimes it appears as a question that will not release its hold.

At the center of all this is an important shift: from event to process, from logic to meaning, from occurrence to interpretation.

That shift leads us to the framework that helps us understand how moral injury develops. Moral Event. Interpretation. Response.

This is the MIR process.

The moral event is the initiating circumstance: the action, decision, witness, omission, or betrayal that carries ethical weight.

Interpretation is the meaning-making process through which the person attempts to understand what the event represents. At first, interpretation often stabilizes. Later, it may deepen, fracture, or become contested.

Response is the ongoing way the person carries the meaning of the event. It includes emotional reactions, behavioral shifts, internal patterns of questioning, and changes in how future situations are approached.

Together, these movements help us see that moral injury is not located in a single moment alone. It unfolds over time through the interaction of what happened, what it comes to mean, and how that meaning is carried.

PART 3—TRACING THE MOMENT

If we return to the moment described earlier—not to relive it, but to understand it—we can begin to trace this process more clearly.

The moral event was the decision made under pressure. It involved competing needs, incomplete information, and a choice that carried consequence. The decision itself was not extraordinary in the context of the work. In many ways, it was ordinary. That is part of what makes such events difficult to recognize. Moral injury does not always begin with the spectacular. It often begins in the ordinary conditions of responsibility.

At the time, the event was experienced as action. Something needed to be done. A judgment had to be made. The moment allowed no space for extended moral reflection. There was urgency. There was necessity. There was movement.

And still, the event carried weight.

It involved responsibility.

It required judgment.

It implicitly raised the question of what mattered most in that moment.

Two needs stood before him. Both were real. Both deserved response. He could not fully answer both. This is crucial. Moral injury often emerges not from deliberate cruelty or obvious wrongdoing, but from conditions in which every available option carries cost. The injury does not require a monstrous action. It may begin in the constrained field of impossible adequacy.

The event itself, however, is not yet the injury.

After the event, interpretation began.

At first, interpretation took the form of stabilization. The mind supplied coherence: I did what I was supposed to do. There was no other option. Anyone would have made the same decision.

These explanations served a real purpose. They protected the continuity of action. They prevented immediate collapse. They allowed the day to continue.

But over time, interpretation shifted.

The question emerged:

Was it right?

This question did not simply challenge the decision. It changed the level at which the decision was being considered. No longer merely procedural, it had become moral. The issue was no longer only whether the choice was justified within the situation. The issue was what the choice meant.

The moment was revisited.

Not as threat.

Not as crisis.

But as meaning.

Why that choice? What did I miss? Was there something else I could have done?

These questions moved the experience from explanation into interpretation. They signaled that the event was now being placed in relation to a broader moral framework.

What mattered most in that moment?

What was I responsible for?

Did I do what was right, or only what was possible?

What choices did I actually have?

What does this say about me?

These questions reveal how interpretation deepens. The event is no longer simply remembered. It is being morally located.

And as interpretation deepens, response begins to take shape.

At first, response appears subtly. The moment returns. It lingers. It resurfaces in quiet spaces. Then it begins to alter other moments. A hesitation where there had once been smooth immediacy. A second-guessing that had not been there before. A greater caution in future decisions. Perhaps even an increased sensitivity to the cost of choosing.

None of this necessarily looks dramatic from the outside.

The person still functions.

They still perform.

They still carry out their responsibilities.

But something has changed in how they carry them.

This is response.

Response is not merely emotion. It is the ongoing form that interpretation takes in the life of the person. It may involve guilt, doubt, anger, caution, withdrawal, defensiveness, overcompensation, or some quieter pattern of internal vigilance. Whatever form it takes, response reflects the attempt to live with the meaning of the event.

Over time, response becomes pattern.

Pattern becomes orientation.

Orientation begins to shape identity.

This is how moral injury becomes formative. Not because a single event possesses magical power, but because the meaning of the event is carried forward into new situations. Interpretation shapes response. Response shapes future interpretation. New events enter the same pattern. The process becomes cumulative.

When we step back, the movement becomes visible:

A moral event occurs.

Interpretation begins—first stabilizing, then deepening.

Response follows—shaping how the experience is carried over time.

This is why moral injury cannot be located in the event alone.

It is located in the movement.

The event matters. But what matters more, for understanding moral injury, is what the event becomes within the person who carries it.

PART 4—NAMING, NOT FIXING

By the time a moment begins to linger, the work has usually already moved on.

There is rarely a clear signal that says: stop here, now, and process what has just occurred. The demands of the role continue. The structure of the day remains intact. Responsibilities do not pause simply because meaning has become unsettled.

This is part of what makes moral injury so difficult to engage.

The experience often goes unaddressed not because it is insignificant, but because there is no obvious cultural or institutional place to put it.

What is needed first is not resolution.

It is recognition.

Recognition begins with noticing that something has remained. That something has not settled. That a particular moment continues to carry weight beyond its immediate occurrence.

Often this begins with simple language:

That didn't sit right.

I keep coming back to that.

Something about that still bothers me.

These are not conclusions. They are openings. They create space for the experience to be acknowledged rather than dismissed.

From there, questions can begin to take shape.

What happened that does not sit right?

What about this no longer makes sense?

What are you still carrying from it?

These questions do not resolve the experience. They locate it. They invite the individual to begin naming where the disturbance is occurring.

This matters because moral injury is not helped by premature reassurance. One of the most common responses to morally difficult experience is to move too quickly toward closure:

You did the best you could.

There was no other option.

You shouldn't feel bad about that.

These statements may be true. They may even become useful later. But when offered too early, they can shut down the deeper work of interpretation. They answer the question before the question has been fully heard.

Moral injury is not addressed by removing tension prematurely.

It is engaged by allowing tension to be explored.

This requires presence.

Not fixing.

Not concluding.

Not racing toward resolution.

But remaining with the question.

Helpful reflection can deepen from initial recognition into more focused exploration:

What changed about what matters here?

What do you feel responsible for?

What feels wrong or unresolved?

What choices were actually available to you?

How has this affected the way you see yourself?

These questions are not a checklist. They are a map. They help trace the shape of the disruption without forcing the experience into a false simplicity.

This work is slow. It should be. Some experiences do not return to clarity. They remain—not as open wounds, but as integrated tensions. The goal is not always to eliminate the weight. It is often to carry it differently.

That movement—from confusion toward understanding, from isolation toward shared language, from fragmentation toward integration—is one of the central tasks in responding to moral injury.

Language makes this possible.

Without language, the experience remains internal. It may be felt intensely, but it remains difficult to communicate. With language, the experience becomes more workable. It can be named. Shared. Reflected upon. Held in conversation without being immediately flattened into explanation.

This is especially important in environments that privilege performance, decisiveness, and resilience. In such environments, moral injury is both more likely to emerge and less likely to be named. The stronger the pressure to remain functional, the easier it becomes to overlook the question that will not settle.

But these moments are not interruptions to the work.

They are part of it.

They reveal that human beings are not only decision-makers. They are meaning-makers. What they do matters, and what what they do comes to mean matters just as much.

Moral injury emerges at the intersection of those realities.

And it asks something difficult of us.

Not quick answers.

Not immediate relief.

But attention.

Honesty.

And a willingness to remain with what does not easily resolve.

REFLECTION

What is a moment that has stayed with you—not because it overwhelmed you, but because it did not settle?

Where have you returned to a decision—not to change it, but to understand it?

What question remains open, even now?

LOOKING AHEAD

We have seen that moral injury is not simply distress or regret.

Next, we will explore the structure beneath it—the moral framework through which experience is interpreted and carried.

Chapter 2

The Moral Framework (M.O.R.A.L)

PART 1—THE LIFE ALREADY SHAPED

He would not have said he was guided by anything like a framework. If someone had asked him how he made decisions, he would have answered in the language he trusted—experience, instinct, training. He would have said that you learn to read a situation quickly, that you pay attention to what is in front of you, that you respond to what is needed. He would not have described it as moral reasoning; he would have described it as doing the work. And that would have been true, as far as it went, but it would not have accounted for what was already shaping him long before any decision was made.

There were patterns he did not notice because they had always been there. Over time, he had learned what mattered—not in a single moment, not through a clear set of instructions, but through repetition. Certain responses were affirmed, certain hesitations corrected. Some outcomes stayed with him because others returned to them—pointing them out, reinforcing them, marking them as significant—while other moments passed without comment and therefore without weight. This is how formation happens: quietly, without announcement.

He learned what to look for, what to respond to first, and what could wait. He learned, without being told directly, that some needs demand immediate attention while others can be deferred, that certain signals carry urgency, that some risks must be addressed before others, and that time is rarely sufficient. None of this felt like learning a system. It felt like learning reality.

When he entered a situation, he did not feel like he was interpreting it; he felt like he was seeing it clearly. Certain details stood out immediately—a shift in tone, a look that indicated something was wrong, a level of urgency that could not be ignored. These things drew his attention without effort and felt obvious, as though anyone would notice them in the same way. But not everything stood out.

Other details remained in the background—not because they were unimportant, but because they did not fit the pattern of what he had learned to prioritize. They did not present themselves as urgent or signal themselves as requiring immediate response, and so they remained unaddressed—not as a failure, but as a consequence of what had been learned.

He did not experience this as limitation. He experienced it as clarity. That clarity allowed him to move quickly, to act without hesitation, and to trust what he saw. He trusted what felt urgent. He trusted the sequence of assessment, prioritization, and response. Over time, this trust became part of how he understood himself: someone who could act, someone who could decide, someone who could carry responsibility.

Because this way of seeing worked, it remained invisible. There was no reason to question it. It allowed him to function effectively in situations that demanded quick judgment and decisive action. It aligned with what others expected and what he expected of himself.

It held—until it didn't.

The moment itself did not announce the shift. It arrived within the flow of responsibility, within the rhythm of decision-making, within the pressure of time and need. There were too many demands and not enough time—there never is. He moved the way he always moved: he assessed, prioritized, and acted. The structure was familiar, the sequence practiced.

But something in the moment did not arrange itself the way it usually did.

Two needs presented themselves, both carrying weight and requiring response. There was no immediate clarity about which should take precedence, no signal that elevated one above the other, no pattern that resolved the tension. He felt it, even if he could not name it.

There was no time to pause, no space to step back and examine the complexity of what was unfolding.

He chose.

The decision came quickly, guided by everything that had been learned and shaped by patterns that had proven reliable in the past. He moved in one direction, acted, and continued. The work did not stop—it never does. From the outside, nothing appeared different. The decision was made, the response carried out, the moment passed.

But something had shifted.

It did not show itself immediately or interrupt his ability to function. He continued to respond to the next need, and the next, and the next. The rhythm of the work continued, and he moved within it without disruption. The moment seemed to settle into the background—just another decision among many.

Until it returned.

Not as a full memory or replay, but as a fragment: the sense of standing between two needs, the movement in one direction, the absence of the other. At first, it surfaced briefly and receded, like other difficult decisions that are acknowledged and absorbed. But it did not remain absorbed.

It came back—not with urgency or accusation, but with persistence. A question formed quietly: Was that the right choice?

He answered the way he knew how. Yes. It followed the pattern, matched the situation, aligned with training. The answer explained the decision, but it did not resolve the experience.

The question remained.

It returned in moments of stillness—when the pace slowed, when there was space to think. It did not interrupt his work, but it stayed with him in a way other decisions had not. He began to notice the difference: other moments passed, this one remained. It did not escalate or overwhelm, but it did not settle.

And in not settling, it began to reveal something he had not previously seen—not just the moment, but the structure through which the moment had been lived.

He began to sense, without fully understanding, that what had guided him was not as simple as he had assumed, that what had felt like clarity might have been more complex, that what had felt inevitable might have been shaped in ways he had never examined. This was not yet a conclusion or even a fully formed thought.

It was a shift—a subtle awareness that the way he saw, chose, and acted had been formed long before the moment arrived, and that something in that formation had now been exposed. Not fully, not clearly—but enough that it could no longer remain entirely unseen.

PART 2—THE STRUCTURE BENEATH MEANING

To understand what began to shift in that moment, it is necessary to examine what had been present all along but remained unseen. The moment did not create the tension he experienced. It revealed a structure that had already been shaping how he perceived, interpreted, and acted within the world.

Human beings do not encounter situations as neutral observers. They encounter them through an interpretive structure that organizes experience before conscious reflection begins. This structure determines what is noticed, what is prioritized, what is felt as urgent, and what is experienced as secondary. It operates prior to deliberate thought, guiding perception in ways that feel immediate and self-evident. What appears obvious is often the result of long formation.

This structure can be described as a moral framework.

A moral framework is not simply a set of beliefs about right and wrong. It is a dynamic system through which meaning is formed, responsibility is understood, judgment is exercised, action is evaluated, and identity is shaped. It operates continuously, often without awareness, providing coherence that allows a person to move through complex environments with a sense of clarity and direction. Because it works most of the time, it remains largely invisible.

It becomes visible when it no longer holds.

The moment he experienced did not simply present competing needs. It disrupted the framework that had previously allowed those needs to be ordered. What had once felt clear became uncertain. What had once been resolved through familiar patterns resisted those patterns. The disruption was not only in the situation. It was in the structure through which the situation was being understood.

To describe this structure more precisely, we can identify five interrelated dimensions through which moral experience is organized: meaning, obligation, right and wrong, agency, and legacy.

Meaning concerns significance. It determines what matters in a given situation and how that significance is ranked. In any moment, multiple elements are present, but only some are experienced as carrying moral weight.

Meaning directs attention, often before conscious reflection begins. It answers the question: What matters here?

This assignment of significance is not neutral. It reflects prior formation—what a person has learned to value, what they have been trained to notice, what has been reinforced through experience. Meaning is both immediate and historical. It is felt in the moment, but shaped across time. In complex situations, meaning becomes strained when multiple elements demand recognition but cannot be fully prioritized without remainder.

Obligation concerns responsibility. It defines what a person believes they are required to carry within a situation. This includes formal responsibility—role expectations, institutional duties—but also internalized responsibility, which may exceed what is explicitly defined. Obligation answers the question: What is mine to do?

Responsibility is rarely singular. It is layered. A person may feel accountable to individuals, systems, outcomes, and values simultaneously. These layers do not always align. One responsibility may be fulfilled at the expense of another. This creates tension not because responsibility is unclear, but because it is present in multiple directions at once. A person may leave a moment knowing they fulfilled one obligation while still feeling they failed another.

Right and wrong concern moral judgment. This dimension provides the criteria through which actions are evaluated. It includes internal standards, professional codes, cultural expectations, and deeply held values. It answers the question: What is the right thing to do?

In straightforward situations, this dimension may appear stable. In complex situations, however, it becomes strained. A person may encounter circumstances in which available options do not align cleanly with established categories. A decision may be justified within one framework while remaining unsettled within another. This does not eliminate judgment; it complicates it. The person is left holding both justification and unease.

Agency concerns capacity. It reflects what a person believes they are able to do within the constraints they face. These constraints may include time, resources, authority, information, and situational pressure. Agency answers the question: What can I do?

Capacity is both actual and perceived. Under pressure, perception of possibility often narrows. Options that may appear visible in hindsight are not always available in the moment. This is not simply a cognitive limitation; it is a feature of operating within constraint. Agency is always exercised within limits, and those limits shape what is seen as possible.

Legacy concerns identity. It reflects how an experience is integrated into a person's understanding of who they are. Legacy is not only about what happened; it is about what what happened comes to mean over time. It answers the question: What does this say about me?

Identity is shaped through repeated interpretation. A single moment may not define a person, but moments that remain unresolved begin to influence how a person understands themselves. Legacy is where the framework becomes personal in its most enduring form. It is where experience moves from event into self-understanding.

These five dimensions do not operate independently. They function as an interconnected system. A shift in one dimension affects the others. When meaning becomes unstable, obligation becomes more difficult to define. When obligation expands, agency may feel insufficient. When agency is constrained, judgments about right and wrong become more complex. When all of these are unsettled, identity becomes implicated.

The framework provides coherence when these dimensions align. It provides tension when they do not.

In the moment he experienced, alignment was disrupted across multiple dimensions. Meaning did not resolve clearly. Obligation was present in more than one direction. Judgment aligned but did not settle. Agency was constrained by circumstance. Identity had not yet been engaged, but it would become implicated over time.

This is why the moment lingered.

It was not simply difficult.

It was structurally unresolved.

The framework that had previously allowed experience to be integrated did not fully hold. The disruption was not visible as a system, but it was felt as tension. That tension did not originate from a single source. It emerged from the interaction of multiple dimensions that could no longer be easily aligned.

Understanding this structure does not eliminate the tension.

It makes it visible.

And visibility is the first step toward engagement.

PART 3—TRACING THE MOMENT

The moment did not present itself as morally complex at the time. It presented as a decision. There was no signal that marked it as different from other decisions he had made, no pause in which the structure of the moment could be examined. It arrived within the rhythm of work, shaped by urgency, constrained by time, and requiring response. It felt familiar in its form, even if something within it resisted clarity.

Two needs were present. Both required attention. Both carried weight.

He moved toward them as he had been trained to do. He assessed quickly, taking in what could be seen and what could be inferred. He registered urgency, evaluated risk, and began to prioritize. This sequence did not require conscious articulation. It unfolded as a practiced response, shaped by repetition and reinforced through experience. Under ordinary conditions, this process produces clarity. In this moment, it did not.

The difficulty did not lie in the absence of information. It lay in the presence of competing significance.

At the level of meaning, both needs appeared to matter. Neither could be dismissed as secondary, and neither clearly outweighed the other. Each carried a form of urgency that demanded recognition. The framework that had previously allowed him to rank significance encountered a situation in which ranking did not resolve easily. The usual signals did not align. What had once felt like a natural ordering of importance now felt unstable.

He still had to choose. The situation did not allow for delay. But the choice did not emerge from clarity. It emerged from constraint.

This is where the first tension formed—not because meaning was absent, but because meaning could not be fully organized. The decision required a prioritization that did not eliminate what remained unaddressed. Something mattered that could not be acted upon. That remainder did not disappear when the choice was made.

From meaning, the moment moved immediately into obligation. What was his to carry in that moment? The answer was not singular. He was responsible for responding to need, responsible for acting within the expectations of his role, responsible for making decisions that aligned with what he had been trained to do, and responsible, in a broader sense, for the well-being of those affected.

These layers of responsibility did not collapse into one another. They remained distinct, each making its own claim. To act in one direction was to fulfill one obligation, but it was also, implicitly, to leave another unfulfilled.

This was not experienced as neglect in the moment, but as necessity. Yet necessity does not erase awareness.

This is where the second tension formed—not because responsibility was unclear, but because it was too present in more than one direction. Obligation exceeded capacity. Even as the decision was made, something of what was owed remained unmet.

From obligation, the moment moved into judgment. What was the right thing to do? Under pressure, judgment often takes the form of rapid alignment. A decision is made that fits within established criteria, and that alignment provides a sense of correctness. In this case, the decision did align with what he had been taught to do. It followed recognizable patterns. It could be explained and defended within the framework of training and expectation.

He chose. He acted.

But alignment did not produce resolution.

The decision was defensible. It was not fully settled.

This reveals the third tension. Judgment, even when justified, did not eliminate moral weight. The framework could account for the decision, but it could not fully absorb its meaning. There was no clear violation, and yet there was no complete sense of rightness. The categories of right and wrong held the decision, but they did not resolve the experience.

From judgment, the moment moved into agency. What could he actually do? The constraints were real. Time was limited. Attention could not be divided equally. Action in one direction required the absence of action in another. Resources were finite. The situation did not allow for a response that addressed everything that mattered.

Within these constraints, the decision was necessary.

But necessity does not remove tension.

Agency defined what was possible. It did not resolve what was carried. The limits of action did not eliminate the awareness of what could not be done. Even as he acted within those limits, the sense of what remained beyond them did not disappear.

This is where the fourth tension formed. The gap between what could be done and what was desired remained. The decision closed one path, but it did not close the awareness of the path not taken. That awareness did not interfere with action in the moment, but it remained available for reflection later.

At the time, the moment ended there. The decision was made. The action was taken. The situation moved forward. The demands of the work continued, and the framework resumed its function. There was no immediate disruption.

But the framework did not resolve with the action.

Later, when the moment returned, the fifth dimension began to take shape: legacy.

What did this moment mean about him?

This question did not appear immediately. It emerged gradually, as the experience resisted integration. The decision, which had been made within the structure of role and expectation, began to be revisited within the structure of identity. The question was no longer only about what happened. It was about what the happening meant.

He began to revisit the decision not only as an action, but as an expression of himself. The choice he made was no longer only about the situation. It began to reflect back on his sense of judgment, his sense of responsibility, and his sense of who he was within the work.

Did I see clearly? Did I choose correctly? Can I trust my own judgment?

These questions did not accuse. They examined. They did not arise from external critique, but from internal reflection. And in that reflection, the moment deepened.

The experience was no longer confined to what happened. It expanded into how what happened was understood.

Across all five dimensions, a pattern can now be seen.

Meaning was present but not fully ordered. Obligation was present in multiple directions. Judgment aligned but did not resolve. Agency constrained what was possible. Legacy began to shape identity.

The moment lingered because each dimension remained active.

Meaning continued to be interpreted. What mattered was still being sorted, still being revisited, still being questioned. Obligation continued to be felt. What was carried did not end when the moment ended. Judgment continued to be evaluated. The decision did not settle into a final category. Agency continued to be reconsidered. What was possible in the moment was re-examined in reflection. Identity continued to be formed. The meaning of the moment extended into the meaning of the self.

The experience did not remain static. It evolved.

Each return to the moment was not a repetition. It was a re-engagement. The framework continued to process what had occurred, attempting to integrate an experience that had not fully settled.

This is why the moment persisted.

It was not simply remembered.

It was unresolved within the structure through which it was being understood.

Tracing the moment in this way reveals that the difficulty does not lie only in the event itself. It lies in how the event moves through the framework. The event initiated the process. The framework carried it forward.

And until the tensions across these dimensions are engaged, the moment remains active—not as interruption, but as presence.

PART 4—WORKING WITHIN THE FRAMEWORK

By the time a moment begins to linger, the decision itself is already past. The action has been taken. The situation has moved forward. Other demands have taken priority. In most environments, there is no natural pause that allows a person to step outside the flow of responsibility and examine what has occurred. The work continues, and the individual continues within it.

What remains is not the moment itself, but the experience of it.

This is where the framework becomes practical.

Not as an abstract concept, but as a way of engaging something that is already being carried. Without structure, the experience often remains diffuse. A person may know that something is unsettled without being able to identify where that unsettledness resides. Everything feels connected, but nothing is clearly defined. The result is a sense of weight without clarity.

The framework provides a way of locating that weight.

The first step is recognition.

Recognition does not require analysis. It begins with noticing that something has not resolved. The language for this is often simple and informal: something about that stayed with me; I keep coming back to it; it didn't sit right. These statements do not explain the experience, but they mark it. They distinguish it from other moments that have passed without remainder.

Recognition is not resolution. It is the acknowledgment that something is still active.

Once the experience is recognized, reflection can begin.

Reflection shifts the focus from a single question—Was that right?—to a set of questions that correspond to different dimensions of the framework. This allows the experience to be examined more fully.

The framework can be engaged through five guiding inquiries:

- What, in that moment, felt like it mattered most?
- What did I experience as my responsibility?
- What about the decision still feels unsettled?
- What did I believe was possible at the time?
- What does this seem to say about me now?

Each question opens a different dimension.

The first engages meaning, allowing the person to revisit how significance was assigned. This often reveals that multiple elements carried weight simultaneously and could not all be addressed. The tension may arise not from failure to care, but from the impossibility of responding fully to everything that mattered.

The second engages obligation, bringing into view the layers of responsibility present in the moment. A person may discover that they were carrying more than was formally required, or that responsibilities were in conflict and could not all be fulfilled.

The third engages judgment, creating space to examine why the decision remains unsettled. This is not an invitation to condemn the decision, but to understand the nature of the moral tension that remains.

The fourth engages agency, allowing the individual to revisit the constraints of the moment. This helps clarify what was actually possible within the conditions that existed, rather than evaluating the decision based solely on hindsight.

The fifth engages legacy, bringing attention to how the experience has been integrated into identity. This dimension often carries the greatest weight because it connects the event to the self.

These questions are not meant to be answered all at once. They are not a checklist. They are a way of entering the experience gradually, allowing each dimension to come into view over time.

As reflection continues, a second movement becomes possible: differentiation.

Without differentiation, the experience remains a single, undivided weight. Everything feels connected and overwhelming. Differentiation allows the individual to distinguish between dimensions. The tension in meaning may be different from the tension in obligation. The tension in judgment may be different from the tension in agency. The tension in identity may be different from all of these.

This distinction does not reduce the experience. It clarifies it.

Clarity changes how the experience is carried. A person may begin to recognize that what feels like failure is actually unresolved obligation, that what feels like confusion is the result of competing meanings, or that what feels like shame is connected to how identity has been shaped by the event.

From differentiation, a third movement emerges: integration.

Integration is not the elimination of tension. It is the ability to place the experience within a broader understanding of oneself and one's work. The moment remains. The decision does not change. The cost, if there was cost, does not disappear.

What changes is how the experience is held.

Instead of remaining undefined, it becomes articulated. Instead of remaining isolated, it becomes shareable. Instead of remaining overwhelming, it becomes more contained.

Integration allows the individual to say: this is what happened; this is where it affected me; this is how I am carrying it.

This does not resolve every question, but it reduces the sense that the experience is unmanageable.

There are also practices that support this process over time.

One is pacing. Not every dimension needs to be explored at once, and not every experience is ready for full articulation immediately. Moving too quickly toward resolution can bypass the depth of the experience. Allowing time for reflection to unfold creates space for more accurate understanding.

Another is relational engagement. While the framework can be used individually, it is often more effective when engaged in conversation. A second person can help reflect what is being said, ask clarifying questions, and provide perspective. However, this requires a particular kind of presence. The goal is not to provide answers. The goal is to support understanding.

Statements that move too quickly toward closure—You did the best you could; There was no other option; You shouldn't feel this way—may contain truth, but when offered prematurely, they can interrupt the deeper work of interpretation.

Remaining with the experience, without forcing it into resolution, allows the framework to become more fully visible.

Finally, it is important to recognize that not all tension will disappear. Some experiences do not resolve completely. Some questions remain open. Some moments continue to carry weight.

Integration does not require the removal of all tension.

It requires the ability to live with tension without being disoriented by it.

This is particularly important in environments where morally complex situations are not rare, but regular. In such environments, the goal cannot be to eliminate moral difficulty. The goal must be to engage it well.

To recognize when a moment has not settled.

To locate where the tension exists.

To reflect across the dimensions of the framework.

To differentiate what is being carried.

To integrate the experience over time.

This is the work of the moral framework.

Not to simplify.

Not to resolve immediately.

But to make visible what is already shaping how the experience is being carried.

REFLECTION

When you return to a moment that has not settled, what do you notice first?

Is it a question of meaning—something that mattered but could not be fully addressed?

Is it a sense of obligation—something you were responsible for that remains unfinished?

Is it a tension in judgment—the feeling that a decision can be explained but not fully resolved?

Is it a question of agency—an awareness of limits that still feels unsettled?

Or is it something deeper—an emerging question about what that moment says about you?

These questions are not meant to be answered quickly. They are not a test of correctness, nor are they a path to immediate resolution. They are a way of locating where the experience continues to live within you.

As you reflect, you may notice that the tension does not sit in only one place. Meaning, obligation, judgment, agency, and identity often overlap,

each shaping how the others are experienced. What feels like confusion may be competing meanings. What feels like failure may be unresolved obligation. What feels like doubt may be a disruption in how judgment has been carried. What feels like limitation may be an encounter with the boundaries of agency. What feels most personal may be the beginning of how identity is being shaped.

The purpose of reflection is not to remove the tension.

It is to understand it.

And understanding begins by allowing the experience to take form—slowly, honestly, without forcing it into conclusions it is not ready to hold.

WHAT'S AHEAD

We now have a way to understand how meaning, obligation, and responsibility shape what is carried.

Next, we will move into process—how moral injury unfolds, is recognized, and begins to take form over time.

Chapter 3

The MIR Process

PART 1—THE MOMENT THAT KEEPS MOVING

At first, it seemed contained. The moment had passed. The decision had been made. The work had continued. There was no immediate disruption, no visible consequence that marked it as different from the many other decisions that filled his days. It took its place among them—another instance of responding under pressure, another example of doing what was required. That is how most moments begin. They end outwardly before they begin inwardly.

In the hours that followed, nothing appeared to change. He moved through the remainder of the day as he always did—responding, assessing, adjusting. The rhythm of the work absorbed him. Each new demand required attention, and attention moved forward rather than back. There was no space to linger, and so he did not. This is often how these moments remain hidden at first—not because they lack significance, but because they are carried within environments that do not pause long enough to register them.

It was later—when the pace slowed, when the structure of the day loosened—that the moment returned. Not fully, not clearly. It surfaced as a fragment, a partial image, a sense rather than a scene. He noticed it without intending to. There was no deliberate act of recall. It appeared in the space where attention was no longer fully occupied. In that space, something from earlier in the day moved forward—not to interrupt, but to remain.

At first, he treated it the way he treated other difficult moments. He explained it. It was the right call. It followed the situation. There was no other option. These explanations were not incorrect. They aligned with how he understood the decision. They fit within the structure that had guided him in the moment. They provided coherence, and for a time, they were enough—but not entirely.

The fragment returned. Not with new information, not with accusation, but with persistence. It appeared again in a different context—driving home, pausing between tasks, sitting in the quiet after the day had ended. Each time, it carried the same quality: incomplete, unresolved, not fully integrated. He began to notice the pattern. This was not a single recollection. It was a returning.

The moment did not remain where it had occurred. It moved. It moved into different parts of his day, into spaces that were not defined by urgency. It appeared when there was time to think, but not necessarily a desire to revisit. It did not demand attention in a forceful way. It simply remained available. This is how these moments begin to unfold over time. They do not stay contained within the original event. They extend beyond it.

The experience was no longer only about what happened. It was about how what happened continued to be present. At first, the presence was subtle—a question, a hesitation, a sense that something had not fully resolved.

Was that the right choice?

He answered the question again. Yes. It followed training. It aligned with expectation. It was what needed to be done. But each time the question returned, the answer felt less complete—not incorrect, but insufficient. The explanation accounted for the decision. It did not settle the experience.

This is where the unfolding begins to shift. The moment is no longer approached only through explanation. It begins to be approached through meaning.

Why does this stay with me?

That question marked a change. It moved the focus from the decision itself to the experience of carrying it. He began to revisit the moment, not to re-decide, but to understand. The sequence remained the same. The facts did not change. But the way he engaged it did.

He noticed details he had not emphasized before—the stillness of the person he did not move toward, the immediacy of the call that pulled him in another direction, the narrowing of time that made hesitation impossible.

These details were not new. They had always been present. But now they were being interpreted differently.

Interpretation does not occur all at once. It develops. At first, it remains close to the event: What happened? What did I do? What else was there? Then it begins to deepen: What did that moment require? What did it reveal? What did I not see? The questions did not accuse. They explored. And in that exploration, something began to take shape.

The moment was not only something that had occurred. It was something that was continuing. This is the nature of the unfolding. A moral moment does not end when the event ends. It continues through interpretation. Each return to the moment is not repetition. It is development. The experience is being worked on, even when it is not being deliberately examined.

He began to notice subtle changes. Nothing dramatic. Nothing that would be visible to others. But present. A hesitation where there had once been immediacy. A second-guessing that lingered longer than before. A quiet questioning of his own judgment.

He still acted. He still responded. He still did the work. But something in how he carried the work had shifted.

This is how the moment moves into response—not as reaction, but as pattern. The experience began to influence how future moments were encountered. It did not prevent action, but it shaped it. It introduced a layer of reflection that had not been present before. It altered the sense of certainty that had once accompanied decision-making.

The moment had become more than an event. It had become a presence. And that presence was not static. It was shaping how he moved forward.

This is the beginning of the MIR process—not as a concept, but as a lived experience. A moment occurs. It is interpreted. That interpretation shapes response. And that response influences what comes next.

The process does not unfold in a straight line. It moves—back and forth, forward and inward, across time. The moment remains not because it has not been explained, but because it has not yet been fully understood.

And until it is engaged at that level, it continues.

Not as interruption—

but as formation.

PART 2—MORAL EVENT, INTERPRETATION, RESPONSE

The unfolding described in the previous section can be understood through a structured process. While the experience itself may feel diffuse, layered, and difficult to locate, it follows a recognizable movement. The MIR process provides language for that movement.

MIR stands for Moral Event, Interpretation, and Response.

These are not rigid stages that occur once and then conclude. They are better understood as interrelated movements within a dynamic system. A person may revisit interpretation long after the event has occurred. A response may reshape how the event is remembered. The process is recursive rather than linear. Even so, distinguishing these movements allows the experience to be examined with greater clarity.

The first movement is the moral event.

A moral event is not simply any difficult or stressful experience. It is an event that carries ethical weight. It involves significance, responsibility, or consequence in a way that engages a person's moral framework. A moral event may take many forms: an action taken under pressure, a decision made between competing goods, a failure to act when action felt necessary, participation in a system that produces harm, or witnessing something that should not have occurred.

What defines the event as moral is not only what happened externally, but how it intersects with the person's sense of what matters, what is required, and what is right. The event presents a situation in which moral meaning is at stake.

At the level of experience, however, the event is often encountered as necessity rather than moral complexity. The individual does not typically pause to analyze ethical dimensions in real time. They respond within the constraints of the moment—time, information, expectation, and role. The event is lived as action before it is understood as meaning.

This distinction is critical.

The event itself does not fully determine what follows.

It creates the conditions for interpretation.

The second movement is interpretation.

Interpretation is the process through which the event is understood. It includes explanation, evaluation, and meaning-making. It is where the individual answers—implicitly or explicitly—the question: What was that?

At first, interpretation often functions to stabilize. It places the event within familiar structures of understanding. The person explains the decision in terms that preserve coherence: it followed protocol, it aligned with training, it was necessary under the circumstances. These interpretations are not superficial; they are essential. They allow the individual to continue functioning without becoming overwhelmed by uncertainty.

But stabilization is not the same as resolution.

If the event is fully integrated at this stage, it does not linger. It becomes part of the person's experience without continuing to demand attention. When the event resists stabilization, however—when the explanations do not fully settle it—interpretation begins to deepen.

This deepening often begins quietly.

The person returns to the event not to reconstruct what happened, but to reconsider what it means. The questions begin to shift. They move from description toward evaluation: Was it right? What did I miss? What did that moment require? What remains unsettled?

Interpretation becomes increasingly moral.

It engages the dimensions described in the previous chapter—meaning, obligation, judgment, agency, and identity. The event is no longer only an occurrence. It becomes a point of tension within the individual's moral framework.

At this stage, interpretation may become unstable.

The explanations that once provided coherence may no longer fully hold. The person may find themselves holding multiple interpretations at the same time: the decision was necessary, and something about it still does not sit right. The situation required action, and something remains unresolved. These are not contradictions in a logical sense. They are indications that the event has exceeded the capacity of a single, stable interpretation.

This is often where moral injury begins to take shape.

Not because the event was extreme, but because its meaning cannot be fully contained within existing frameworks.

The third movement is response.

Response refers to how the interpreted event is carried forward. It includes emotional, cognitive, relational, and behavioral patterns that emerge as the person attempts to live with what has occurred. Response is not limited to immediate reaction; it is ongoing. It develops over time as interpretation continues to evolve.

If interpretation centers on unresolved responsibility, response may include increased vigilance, over-functioning, or difficulty setting limits. If interpretation centers on uncertainty in judgment, response may involve hesitation, second-guessing, or diminished confidence. If interpretation engages identity, response may include self-questioning or a shift in how the person understands themselves.

These responses are not arbitrary.

They are structured.

They reflect the meaning the event has taken on.

This is a crucial insight of the MIR process: response is not simply a reaction to the event. It is a continuation of interpretation. The way a person carries the experience is shaped by how they have come to understand it.

Over time, response patterns can become self-reinforcing.

A person who becomes more cautious in decision-making may encounter future situations differently. That altered approach may generate new experiences that confirm the initial interpretation. A person who assumes greater responsibility may carry more than is required, reinforcing a sense of obligation that exceeds actual capacity. In this way, the MIR process extends beyond a single event into ongoing formation.

This is why moral injury is not best understood as a single occurrence.

It is a process.

It unfolds through repeated engagement between event, interpretation, and response.

Understanding this process also opens pathways for repair.

Repair does not begin by eliminating the event. The event cannot be undone. Instead, repair engages the movements where the experience remains active. It may involve clarifying the nature of the moral event, recognizing where interpretation has become overly rigid or incomplete, and identifying response patterns that have developed.

Repair is not the imposition of a new interpretation for the sake of relief.

It is the careful re-examination of what has been carried.

This may include differentiating between actual responsibility and perceived responsibility, acknowledging constraints that were present in the moment, or allowing space for moral grief rather than attempting to resolve the experience through explanation alone.

The goal is not to simplify the experience.

It is to make it more accurately understood.

When the MIR process becomes visible, the experience becomes more navigable. The person is no longer dealing with an undefined sense that something is wrong. They can begin to see where the tension originates, how it has developed, and how it is being carried forward.

Moral Event.

Interpretation.

Response.

These movements do not remove complexity.

They reveal it in a way that allows it to be engaged.

PART 3—FOLLOWING THE DEVELOPMENT OF MORAL INJURY

To understand the MIR process fully, it is necessary to follow a morally significant moment as it unfolds over time. This is not an abstract exercise. It is a way of observing how an event becomes something more than an event—how action becomes interpretation, and how interpretation becomes something that is carried forward.

The moral event begins under pressure.

There is no extended deliberation and no opportunity to pause and map the ethical structure of the situation. Two needs present themselves, both real, both urgent, both requiring response. Time is limited, information is partial, and responsibility is immediate. The situation does not invite reflection. It requires action.

He does what he has been trained to do.

He assesses quickly, identifying what appears most urgent. He prioritizes, drawing on patterns that have guided him before. He acts, moving in one direction while leaving another unaddressed. The decision is not careless and not uninformed. It is shaped by experience, expectation, and the constraints of the moment.

At this point, the event is experienced primarily as necessity.

There is no internal signal that marks it as something that will remain. It is one decision among many. It carries weight, but not yet in a way that separates it from the flow of other decisions. The work continues, and the event recedes into the background of ongoing activity.

This is the first important observation.

Moral injury does not begin with immediate disruption.

It begins within function.

The person continues to act, continues to respond, continues to meet the demands of the situation. The event is contained within the structure of the work, and for a time, it appears to remain there.

Then the moment returns.

Not dramatically and not all at once. It surfaces in fragments—an image, a question, a sensation of incompleteness. The return is not yet analysis. It is presence. The event, which seemed to have passed, begins to reappear within the individual's ongoing experience.

This is where interpretation begins to move beyond stabilization.

Initially, interpretation takes a familiar form. He explains the decision in terms that preserve coherence: it followed training, it aligned with expectations, it was the best available option under the circumstances. These explanations are necessary. They allow the event to remain intelligible and prevent immediate destabilization.

But the return of the moment signals that these explanations are not sufficient.

The event has not fully integrated.

This marks the transition from surface interpretation to deeper interpretation.

The questions begin to shift.

What happened becomes: What did that moment require?

Why that decision becomes: What did I not address?

What I did becomes: What does that say about what mattered?

Interpretation moves from description toward meaning.

At this stage, the event begins to engage the moral framework more fully. Meaning becomes unstable as the person recognizes that more than one thing mattered in the moment. Obligation becomes layered as multiple responsibilities come into view. Judgment becomes unsettled as the decision, though defensible, does not feel fully resolved. Agency is reconsidered as the constraints of the moment are revisited. Identity begins to emerge as the person reflects on what the decision suggests about themselves.

The event is no longer a closed occurrence.

It becomes an open question.

From this deepening interpretation, response begins to take shape.

At first, response is subtle.

A hesitation in similar situations.

A second-guessing that lingers longer than before.

A heightened awareness of what might be missed.

These changes do not disrupt function, but they indicate that the event is no longer contained. It is influencing how future moments are encountered. The person continues to act, but action is now shaped by what remains unresolved.

As interpretation continues, response patterns become more defined.

If the person begins to interpret the event as a failure to meet responsibility, response may take the form of overcompensation. They may carry more than is required in future situations, attempting to ensure that nothing is left unaddressed. This is not simply increased diligence. It is an attempt to resolve an unresolved sense of obligation.

If interpretation centers on uncertainty in judgment, response may involve hesitation. Decisions that were once made quickly now take longer. The person may revisit options repeatedly, seeking a level of certainty that is not available. Confidence in their own judgment begins to erode—not because they lack ability, but because the framework through which judgment operates has been unsettled.

If interpretation engages identity, response may become more internal. The person may begin to question what the moment reveals about who they are. This is not always expressed directly. It may appear as a quiet distancing from previous confidence, a subtle shift in self-understanding that remains beneath the surface of ongoing performance.

These response patterns are not independent of interpretation.

They are shaped by it.

This is the central dynamic of the MIR process.

The event initiates.

Interpretation develops.

Response carries.

And then response feeds back into interpretation.

A person who becomes more hesitant may interpret future moments through that hesitation. A person who assumes greater responsibility may perceive obligation more expansively. A person who questions their identity may approach future decisions with a different sense of self. The process becomes cumulative.

The original event is no longer the only factor shaping experience.

The responses that have developed begin to influence how new events are interpreted.

In this way, moral injury extends beyond a single moment into an ongoing pattern of perception and response.

This is why some experiences remain active long after they occur.

The event has ended.

The process has not.

Each return to the moment is not repetition.

It is continuation.

The person is not simply remembering.

They are still interpreting.

They are still responding.

They are still being shaped.

This does not mean that the process is fixed.

It means that it is active.

And what is active can be engaged.

Tracing the development of moral injury through MIR reveals that the difficulty does not lie solely in what happened. It lies in how what happened continues to move through interpretation and response over time.

The event is the beginning.

Interpretation gives it form.

Response gives it continuity.

And together, they shape how the person carries not only that moment, but every moment that follows.

PART 4—ASSESSING THE PROCESS, IDENTIFYING THE PATTERN

By the time a moral moment begins to linger, the event itself is no longer the primary issue.

The decision has already been made. The action has already been taken. The situation has already moved forward. What remains active is not the event itself, but the process through which it is being carried. This is why returning only to the facts of the situation rarely resolves the tension. The facts may be clear. The meaning is not.

The MIR process provides a way of locating where that meaning remains unsettled and how it continues to shape the person who carries it.

The first step is to identify the moral event with clarity.

This requires moving beyond general descriptions of difficulty into specific articulation. It is not enough to say that something was hard or that a situation was stressful. The question is whether the event carried moral weight. Did it involve a decision that mattered? Did it engage responsibility in a way that could not be fully satisfied? Did it require choosing between competing goods or acting within constraints that left something unresolved?

Naming the event anchors the process.

Without this level of clarity, the experience remains diffuse, and what is being carried cannot be fully engaged. When the event is named, the individual can begin to distinguish between what happened and how it is being carried.

The second step is to examine interpretation.

How is the event being understood now?

This question often reveals that interpretation has already taken shape, even if it has not been explicitly articulated. A person may be carrying conclusions they have never clearly stated. These conclusions often take the form of assumptions: I should have done more. I missed something. I failed in some way. I cannot trust my own judgment. Something about that moment does not make sense.

Interpretation is rarely neutral.

It is often partial.

It may emphasize one dimension of the experience while neglecting others. A person may interpret the event primarily through obligation, assuming responsibility that exceeds what was actually possible. They may interpret through judgment, focusing on whether the decision was right or wrong without adequately considering the constraints that shaped it. They may interpret through identity, allowing a single moment to carry disproportionate weight in defining who they are.

Examining interpretation does not mean correcting it immediately.

It means making it visible.

The third step is to identify response.

How has the interpretation been carried forward?

Response often becomes visible through patterns. A person may notice that they return to the same moment repeatedly, that they hesitate in situations that resemble the original event, or that they carry a heightened sense of responsibility that extends beyond what is required. These patterns are not random. They are structured responses shaped by interpretation.

Several response patterns appear frequently within the MIR process.

One pattern is re-examination.

The person returns to the moment again and again, reviewing details, reconsidering decisions, and searching for a resolution that has not yet been found. This is not simply memory. It is an attempt to complete an interpretation that remains unfinished. The person is not trying to recall the event more accurately. They are trying to understand it more fully.

Another pattern is over-responsibility.

The individual begins to carry more than is required in future situations. They may anticipate needs more aggressively, assume obligations that extend beyond their role, or feel responsible for outcomes that are not fully within their control. This pattern often emerges when interpretation centers on unresolved obligation. The person attempts to prevent recurrence by expanding what they carry.

A third pattern is hesitation.

Decision-making becomes slower, more cautious, and more deliberate. The person may find it difficult to trust their own judgment, even in situations where they previously acted with confidence. This does not necessarily reflect a loss of skill. It reflects a disruption in the framework through which judgment is made. The person is no longer certain that alignment between action and meaning will occur.

Another pattern is withdrawal.

The individual may begin to create distance from situations that resemble the original event. This is not always overt avoidance. It may appear as a subtle shift in preference toward roles or tasks that reduce exposure to morally complex decisions. The goal is not disengagement from work, but protection from unresolved tension.

Finally, there is identity disturbance.

The event begins to shape how the person understands themselves. This is not always expressed directly. It may appear as a quiet shift in self-perception: I am not as clear as I thought I was. I am not as capable as I believed. I am not sure who I am in this work anymore. This pattern often carries the greatest weight because it extends beyond action into self-understanding.

These patterns are not mutually exclusive.

They often overlap.

A person may re-examine the moment while also carrying increased responsibility. They may hesitate in decisions while also questioning their identity. The patterns interact, reinforcing one another and shaping how future experiences are encountered.

The purpose of identifying these patterns is not to categorize the person.

It is to clarify the process.

When the patterns are visible, the experience becomes more structured. The individual can begin to see that what they are carrying is not random or inexplicable. It follows a movement. It has internal logic.

This clarity creates the possibility of response that is intentional rather than reactive.

At this point, a fourth step becomes possible: identifying direction.

Where might engagement begin?

If the event has not been clearly named, the work may begin there. If interpretation is rigid or incomplete, the work may involve expanding how the event is understood. If response patterns are dominant, the work may involve recognizing how those patterns developed and what they are attempting to accomplish.

For example, over-responsibility may be understood not simply as excess, but as an effort to resolve an unresolved sense of obligation. Re-examination may be seen not as fixation, but as an attempt to complete interpretation. Hesitation may be recognized as a response to disrupted judgment rather than as indecision. Identity disturbance may be understood as an effort to integrate an experience that has not yet found its place within the self.

This reframing does not eliminate the patterns.

It situates them.

And when patterns are situated, they can be engaged.

Engagement does not mean immediate resolution.

It means entering the process with awareness.

A person can begin to ask:

What part of this experience remains most active?

Is it the event itself, still unnamed?

Is it the interpretation, still unsettled?

Is it the response, now shaping how I move forward?

These questions do not force conclusions.

They guide attention.

The goal of MIR assessment is not to simplify moral complexity.

It is to prevent that complexity from remaining unstructured.

When the process is visible, the person is no longer only experiencing tension. They are understanding it. They can locate it. They can begin to work with it rather than being shaped by it without awareness.

This is where the possibility of repair begins.

Not in eliminating the event.
Not in forcing resolution.
But in bringing the process into view.

REFLECTION

When you think of a moment that continues to return, can you name the event clearly?

How have you been interpreting it?

What patterns of response have developed around that interpretation?

Do you find yourself returning to the moment, carrying more than is required, hesitating in similar situations, withdrawing from complexity, or questioning your own sense of self?

Which of these feels most present?

And where, within that process, does the experience feel most active now?

LOOKING AHEAD

We have seen how moral injury emerges through recognition, impact, and rupture.

Next, we will examine the different pathways through which it develops—how people come to carry what does not resolve.

Chapter 4

Pathways of Moral Injury

PART 1—THE WEIGHT OF WHAT WAS DONE

HE DID NOT THINK of it as a line crossed—not at the time. There was no moment where he paused and recognized that something had shifted in a permanent way. No internal declaration. No sense that this decision would mark him differently than the others. It came the way many decisions come—within pressure, within expectation, within the narrowing of time that allows only one direction to be taken. He acted. That was all.

The situation did not allow for distance. It required proximity—attention directed toward what was in front of him, toward what needed to be done, toward what could not wait. There was movement, urgency, and the steady compression of options that happens when time closes in around a decision. He did not experience himself as choosing between right and wrong. He experienced himself as choosing between what could be done and what could not.

There were reasons. There are always reasons.

He could account for them even as he moved. He could feel the logic of the situation as it unfolded—the necessity, the constraint, the alignment with what he had been trained to recognize as appropriate response. There was no sense of acting outside the bounds of what was expected. If anything, there was a sense of moving within them, following the structure that had been built into him over time. The decision came quickly because it had to, and once it was made, there was no pause. He moved forward. The work continued.

From the outside, nothing marked the moment as different. The action was taken. The sequence advanced. Other needs presented themselves, and he responded to them in turn. The environment did not shift to acknowledge what had happened. There was no signal that something of lasting significance had occurred. It was absorbed, as everything else was absorbed. This is how many of these moments are carried at first—they are completed within action and do not linger immediately because there is no space for them to linger.

Later, when the pace slowed, he remembered what he had done. Not all at once, and not in a way that reconstructed the full scene. It came back in pieces—the movement of his hands, the direction he had taken, the choice that had been made without hesitation. At first, it did not feel different from other memories. It was something that had happened, something that could be recalled, placed within the sequence of the day, and then set aside. He did not question it, because there was no immediate reason to.

He understood why he had acted. He could explain it. It followed the situation. It matched what was required. It was the best available option. These explanations held—for a time—but something about the moment did not remain where it had been placed.

It returned. Not as a question, not yet, but as a presence.

He began to notice it in the spaces where nothing else demanded his attention. In those moments, the memory did not come forward as a narrative. It came forward as a sensation—something slightly out of alignment, something not fully settled. He did not immediately recognize what it was, only that it remained. He revisited the moment again, this time more deliberately, replaying what he had done and tracing the sequence more carefully while paying attention to details that had not seemed significant before.

He noticed the precision of his action, the absence of hesitation, and the way the decision had felt immediate and necessary. Nothing in the sequence appeared incorrect, and yet something did not sit. This was the first shift—not in the memory itself, but in how it was experienced. He began to feel the moment differently than he had understood it.

This is where the pathway begins.

The event itself had not changed. What had changed was the space around it. At first, he approached it the way he approached everything else. He explained it: I did what I had to do. There was no other option. Anyone in that situation would have done the same. These statements were not false. They were grounded in the reality of the moment. They reflected the constraints, the expectations, the conditions under which the decision had been made.

But they did not fully contain the experience.

The more he returned to the moment, the more he noticed something else emerging—not as contradiction, but as addition. Yes, it was necessary, and it carried something. He could not yet name what that something was, only that it remained. He began to sense that the moment was not only about what had been done, but about what that action now meant.

This shift was subtle. It did not interrupt his work. It did not prevent him from acting in future situations. It did not announce itself in a way that demanded immediate attention. But it was there—a quiet awareness that the decision, while justified, was not neutral, and that something in the act itself had weight. Not because it was wrong in any clear sense, but because it had crossed into something that could not be entirely explained by necessity.

He began to notice that the memory did not behave like other memories. It did not simply pass. It held its place in his attention longer than expected, returned without invitation, and remained present even after it had been explained. In that persistence, it began to take on a different kind of significance—not as an event that needed to be corrected, and not as a mistake that could be undone, but as something that had become part of him.

This is how the pathway of action begins to form—not at the moment of decision, but in what follows.

The realization does not arrive all at once. It develops. He found himself returning to a question he had not asked before: What did I just do? The question was not about the mechanics of the action—those were clear. It was about the meaning. What had been required of him? What had he participated in? What had the action made possible—or prevented?

The answers did not come easily, because the moment could be justified and still not fully settled. He began to recognize something he had not previously considered—that it is possible to do what is necessary and still carry it.

This recognition did not accuse him. It did not assign blame. But it changed how the moment lived within him. The action was no longer only something he had done. It was something he was now carrying, and that distinction mattered.

Because carrying is not the same as completing.

The moment had ended, but it had not finished. It remained—not as interruption, but as weight. That weight did not come from uncertainty about the facts. It came from something deeper—something not yet named, but already shaping how he remembered, how he reflected, and how he would move forward.

PART 2—THE FOUR PATHWAYS

Moral injury does not arise from a single kind of experience. While the MIR process describes how morally significant moments unfold over time, it does not specify the forms those moments take. To understand moral injury more fully, it is necessary to examine the recurring pathways through which moral events most often occur.

These pathways are not exhaustive, but they are widely observed across contexts. They provide a way of recognizing the structure of morally injurious experience as it is happening, rather than only in retrospect. The four primary pathways are action, inaction, witness, and betrayal.

Each pathway describes a different relationship between the individual and the morally significant event. Each engages the moral framework in distinct ways. And each produces its own characteristic tensions in interpretation and response.

The first pathway is action.

This pathway involves participating in or carrying out an act that conflicts, in some way, with one's moral framework. The conflict may be clear at the time, or it may only become apparent later through reflection. In some cases, the action is taken under direct instruction or within institutional expectation. In others, it emerges from necessity, where no available option aligns fully with what the individual believes is right.

What distinguishes this pathway is not simply that something was done, but that what was done carries moral weight that does not resolve easily. The individual may be able to justify the action. They may be able to explain why it was necessary, why it aligned with training, or why no better alternative was available. And yet, the act itself remains present in a way that exceeds explanation.

This pathway often engages interpretation at the level of judgment and identity. The person may ask: Was that right? What kind of person does that? Even when the action is defensible, it may not feel neutral. The tension does not come from uncertainty about what happened. It comes from the meaning of having done it.

The second pathway is inaction.

This pathway involves not doing something that, in retrospect, feels morally significant. It may involve being unable to act, failing to act in time, or choosing one course of action that leaves another unaddressed. Inaction often occurs within constraint. Time, resources, authority, or information may limit what is possible. The individual may have been aware of these constraints in the moment, and the decision not to act may have been reasonable within those limits.

However, in reflection, the focus often shifts from constraint to possibility.

The person may begin to ask: What if I had done more? What if I had seen it differently? What if I had acted sooner? These questions do not always reflect what was actually possible. They reflect the expansion of interpretation over time, as the event is revisited outside the conditions in which it occurred.

Inaction often engages interpretation at the level of obligation. The tension centers on what was not carried, what responsibility feels unmet, and what remains unfinished. The individual may not be questioning what they did. They may be questioning what they did not do.

The third pathway is witness.

This pathway involves observing or being present for something that conflicts with one's moral framework, without being able to prevent it. The individual is not the primary actor, but they are not removed from the event. They are close enough to see, to understand, and to register that something has occurred that should not have occurred.

Witnessing can be particularly complex because it involves a form of participation without direct action. The person may feel implicated simply by being present. They may question their own role, even if they had limited or no capacity to intervene. The event becomes part of their experience, not because they caused it, but because they encountered it in a way that cannot be dismissed.

This pathway often engages interpretation at the level of judgment and agency. The person may ask: Should this have happened? Could I have done anything? What does it mean that I saw it and it still happened? The tension arises not only from the event itself, but from the perceived relationship between the individual and the event.

The fourth pathway is betrayal.

This pathway involves a perceived violation of trust by an individual, institution, or system that the person relied upon. Betrayal may occur when leaders make decisions that conflict with stated values, when systems fail to protect those they are responsible for, or when expectations of integrity are not met. The individual experiences not only the event itself, but the breakdown of the structure that was supposed to guide and support action.

Betrayal introduces a different kind of disruption.

It is not only about what happened.

It is about who was supposed to prevent it.

The individual may feel that they acted within a system that did not hold. They may question whether they were placed in a position where harm was unavoidable. They may experience anger, disillusionment, or a loss of trust—not only in others, but in the structures that once provided coherence.

This pathway often engages interpretation at the level of meaning and trust. The person may ask: What was I part of? What did I believe that no longer holds? What does it mean that the system I relied on failed?

While these pathways are distinct, they are not mutually exclusive.

A single event may involve more than one pathway. A person may act in a way that feels morally complex while also witnessing something they could not prevent. They may experience inaction within a system that later feels like betrayal. These pathways often overlap, creating layered experiences that engage multiple dimensions of the moral framework simultaneously.

Understanding the pathways does not simplify the experience.

It clarifies its structure.

When a person can recognize the pathway through which a moral event has occurred, they gain language for what they are carrying. They can begin to distinguish between different forms of moral tension rather than experiencing them as a single, undifferentiated weight.

This distinction matters.

The interpretation of an action-based event differs from the interpretation of an inaction-based event. The response patterns associated with witnessing differ from those associated with betrayal. Without recognizing the pathway, a person may attempt to resolve one form of tension using the language of another, leading to further confusion.

The pathways also shape how the MIR process unfolds.

The moral event is structured differently depending on the pathway. Interpretation engages different dimensions of the moral framework. Response patterns emerge in ways that reflect the specific nature of the experience. By identifying the pathway, the individual can more accurately locate where the process is active and what kind of engagement may be needed.

This is not about categorizing experience for its own sake.

It is about making experience more visible.

When the pathway is named, the event becomes more specific. When the event becomes more specific, interpretation can become more precise. When interpretation becomes more precise, response can be better understood.

Clarity does not remove moral complexity.

But it allows complexity to be engaged.

PART 3—TRACING THE PATHWAYS

To understand the four pathways fully, it is necessary to follow a single scenario as it unfolds across them. Not because every event will include all four pathways, but because seeing them together reveals how moral injury often develops in layered and overlapping ways.

The situation begins as many do—with urgency.

A call comes in. The details are incomplete, but the severity is clear enough. There are multiple individuals involved, competing needs, and limited time to respond. The environment shifts quickly into coordinated action. Roles are assumed. Movement begins. The structure of response takes over.

He enters the situation as part of that structure.

His responsibility is defined, at least initially. He knows where to focus, what to assess, and how to proceed. The first moments are driven by necessity. There is no space to consider the broader implications of what is unfolding. There is only the immediate demand: respond.

Within that demand, the first pathway emerges—action.

A decision is required. There is no option that fully satisfies what the situation demands. He must choose a course that prioritizes one need over another. The decision is made quickly, guided by training and shaped by the constraints of time and information. He acts. The action is not careless. It is not uninformed. It is necessary.

At this stage, the event is contained within the logic of response.

The action aligns with expectation. It fits within the framework of what should be done. It can be explained. But even here, something begins to form. The action carries weight—not because it is clearly wrong, but because it involves consequence that cannot be fully accounted for within the moment.

The second pathway emerges alongside the first—in this case, inaction.

The action taken requires something else to be left undone. There is no capacity to address every need simultaneously. One direction is chosen, and another is not. In the moment, this is understood as necessity. The constraints are clear. The decision reflects what is possible.

But the unaddressed need does not disappear.

It remains present as absence.

At first, this absence is not experienced as failure. It is simply part of the structure of the situation. The work continues. Other actions follow. The sequence advances. The event appears to remain contained.

Then the moment begins to settle.

And in that settling, the unaddressed need becomes more visible.

The person begins to revisit what was not done. Not as a factual reconstruction, but as a moral question. Could something else have been possible? Was there a different way to see the situation? Did I miss something? The pathway of inaction becomes more prominent in interpretation than it was in the moment itself.

The third pathway—witness—emerges through proximity.

During the response, he is aware of things that are not directly within his control. He sees outcomes that he did not produce but cannot prevent. He observes interactions, conditions, or consequences that do not align with what should happen. In the moment, this awareness is secondary. It is registered, but not engaged. The priority remains action.

Later, this changes.

The memory of what was witnessed begins to separate from the memory of what was done. The individual recalls not only their own actions, but what they were present for. The sense of proximity becomes more significant. The question is no longer only: What did I do? It becomes: What did I see, and what does it mean that I saw it?

This is where witness begins to carry weight.

The individual may recognize that they were not responsible for what occurred, but they were not removed from it either. They were there. They understood what was happening. And that awareness becomes part of what is carried.

The fourth pathway—betrayal—emerges more slowly.

It is not always present in the moment. It often develops through reflection, as the individual begins to consider the broader context in which the event occurred. Questions begin to shift outward. What structures shaped this situation? What expectations were set? What support was available or absent? What should have been in place that was not?

In this scenario, the individual may begin to recognize that the conditions of the situation were not only the result of immediate factors. They may see that the system within which they were operating did not fully hold. Resources may have been insufficient. Communication may have been incomplete. Leadership decisions may have contributed to the constraints that made the moment what it was.

This recognition does not erase personal responsibility.

But it complicates it.

The individual begins to experience the event not only as something they participated in, but as something they were placed within. The question shifts again: What was I part of? What should have been different before I ever arrived?

This is the movement of betrayal—not always as a dramatic violation, but as a growing awareness that the structures relied upon did not fully support what was required.

Across these four pathways, the event becomes layered.

Action carries the weight of what was done. Inaction carries the weight of what was not done. Witness carries the weight of what was seen. Betrayal carries the weight of the system in which it all occurred.

These layers do not remain separate.

They interact.

The individual may begin to interpret their action through the lens of inaction: I chose one thing, but I left something else. They may interpret their inaction through the lens of witness: I saw what was happening and could not change it. They may interpret both through the lens of betrayal: I was operating within a system that made this outcome more likely.

The experience becomes more complex, not less.

This complexity is not confusion.

It is accumulation.

Each pathway adds a dimension to the moral weight of the event. What began as a single decision becomes a multi-layered experience that engages meaning, obligation, judgment, agency, and identity in different ways.

This is where the MIR process becomes particularly important.

The moral event is no longer singular. It is composed of multiple pathways. Interpretation must now account for each of these layers. Response patterns begin to reflect the combined weight of action, inaction, witness, and betrayal.

The individual may re-examine the event repeatedly, attempting to understand how these layers fit together. They may carry increased responsibility, trying to account for what was done and not done. They may hesitate in future situations, aware of the complexity that can emerge within a single moment. They may question their place within the system that shaped the event.

The process is no longer simple.

But it is not random.

It follows structure.

Tracing the pathways reveals that moral injury often develops not from a single dimension of experience, but from the interaction of multiple dimensions. The event becomes injurious not because it was one kind of thing, but because it became many things at once.

This is why naming the pathways matters.

It allows the individual to see the components of what they are carrying.

Not as a single, undifferentiated weight—

but as a structured experience that can be examined.

And what can be examined can begin to be understood.

PART 4—IDENTIFYING THE PATHWAY, ENGAGING THE WORK

By the time a moral moment begins to take shape over time, the experience is rarely singular. What remains is not only what happened, but how what happened is being carried across multiple dimensions. The individual may feel a general sense that something is unresolved, but without structure, that sense remains diffuse—experienced as weight without clarity, persistence without location.

The four pathways—action, inaction, witness, and betrayal—provide a way of locating that experience. They do not simplify what has occurred, but they make it more specific.

The first step in engaging the pathways is identification. This begins with a straightforward but often overlooked question: What kind of experience was this? Was there something I did that now carries weight? Was there something I did not do that continues to remain with me? Was there something I witnessed that I cannot fully set aside? Was there something about the system or structure that feels like it did not hold?

These questions are not mutually exclusive. More than one pathway may be present, and in many cases that is precisely what creates the complexity.

A person may initially focus on action—what they did—only to realize that inaction is also present—what they were unable to do. They may recognize that witnessing adds another layer, that being present for something they could not change continues to carry significance. They may then begin to see that the situation itself was shaped by conditions that feel, in retrospect, like a form of betrayal.

The experience expands.

Without a way of naming these layers, they remain fused together. Everything feels like one problem. The pathways allow the individual to begin separating what has been combined.

This is the second step: differentiation.

Differentiation does not reduce the weight of the experience; it clarifies its structure. What belongs to action is not the same as what belongs to inaction. What belongs to witness is not the same as what belongs to betrayal. Each pathway carries a distinct kind of tension.

Action often carries the weight of participation. Inaction carries the weight of absence. Witness carries the weight of proximity. Betrayal carries the weight of broken expectation.

When these are not distinguished, the individual may attempt to resolve one kind of tension using the language of another. A person may carry the weight of inaction but interpret it as action, experiencing themselves as having done something wrong rather than as having been unable to do everything that was required. A person may carry the weight of betrayal but internalize it as personal failure, assuming responsibility for conditions shaped by factors beyond their control.

Differentiation allows these misalignments to become visible, and that visibility changes how the experience can be engaged.

The third step is examining how each pathway is being interpreted.

Once the pathways are identified, the individual can begin to ask: What meaning has this pathway taken on? If the pathway is action, how is the act being understood? Is it seen as necessary, as wrong, as unresolved, or as something that resists clear classification? If the pathway is inaction, how is the absence being interpreted? Is it being understood within the constraints of the moment, or is it being expanded into a sense of total responsibility?

If the pathway is witness, what does the individual believe about their proximity to the event? Do they see themselves as responsible, as powerless, or as something in between? If the pathway is betrayal, how is the system being understood? Is the failure located externally, or has it been internalized?

These interpretations shape everything that follows. They determine how the experience is carried.

This leads to the fourth step: identifying response patterns within each pathway.

Each pathway tends to produce characteristic forms of response. Action may lead to self-examination, moral questioning, or a sustained effort to understand the meaning of what was done. Inaction may lead to over-responsibility—an attempt to carry more in future situations to compensate for what feels unfinished. Witness may lead to a persistent return to what was seen, an effort to make sense of proximity without agency. Betrayal may lead to anger, disillusionment, or a loss of trust in structures that once provided coherence.

These responses are not random. They are structured. They represent attempts to resolve what remains unresolved within each pathway.

When these responses are not identified, they may begin to shape behavior without awareness. A person may become more vigilant, more hesitant, more withdrawn, or more burdened without fully understanding why. Over time, these patterns begin to feel like part of the self rather than responses to a specific experience.

Identifying the pathway brings those patterns into view. The individual can begin to recognize: This is not all of me. This is how I am carrying this.

That distinction matters, because it creates the possibility of engagement.

The final step is direction.

Where does the work begin?

If the pathway of action is dominant, the work may involve engaging the meaning of what was done—not to undo it, but to understand how it fits within the individual's moral framework. If the pathway of inaction is most active, the work may involve revisiting the constraints of the moment and differentiating between what was possible and what is now being imagined in retrospect.

If the pathway of witness is central, the work may involve acknowledging the impact of proximity without collapsing it into responsibility. If the pathway of betrayal is most significant, the work may involve locating where trust was broken and how that disruption is being carried internally.

These are not solutions.

They are entry points.

The goal is not to resolve the experience immediately. It is to engage it accurately. Accuracy changes how the experience is held.

Instead of remaining a single, overwhelming weight, it becomes a structured reality that can be examined, understood, and gradually integrated.

The pathways do not remove moral complexity. They reveal its form.

And when that form is visible, the experience can be carried differently—not because the past has changed, but because the person is no longer carrying it without structure.

REFLECTION

When you return to a moment that continues to stay with you, which pathway feels most present?

Is it something you did, something you could not do, something you witnessed, or something about the system that did not hold?

Where might more than one pathway be present?

How have these pathways shaped the way you are interpreting the experience now?

And what patterns of response have developed as a result?

LOOKING AHEAD

We have encountered the primary ways moral injury takes shape.

Next, we will examine the conditions that intensify it—especially the role of certainty, control, and the assumptions we rely on.

Chapter 5

Certainty, Control, and the Illusion of Stability

PART 1—THE NEED FOR THINGS TO MAKE SENSE

He did not think of himself as someone who needed certainty. If asked, he might have said the opposite. The work had taught him that things rarely unfold as expected, that plans shift, that outcomes cannot always be controlled. He had learned to adapt, to respond, to move within uncertainty without becoming paralyzed by it. Flexibility was part of competence. Control, in the absolute sense, had never been the goal.

And yet, there was something he had come to rely on.

It was not control over events. It was control over meaning.

He did not name it that way. It did not present itself as a need. It was simply how things worked. When something happened, it could be understood. When a decision was made, it could be explained. When an outcome unfolded, it could be placed within a structure that made sense of it. This did not eliminate difficulty, but it made difficulty navigable. There was a way things fit together.

Even when the situation was complex, even when the outcome was not what anyone wanted, there was still a sense that it could be interpreted—that it could be located within a framework of cause and effect, responsibility and response, action and consequence. This was the stability he carried: not that everything would go according to plan, but that everything could be made to make sense.

Over time, this expectation became so integrated that he no longer recognized it as an expectation. It felt like reality. It felt like the way things were—until it didn't.

The moment did not begin as disruption. It began as something familiar: a situation unfolding under pressure, information incomplete, time limited, decisions required. He entered into it the way he always did—attentive, responsive, oriented toward what needed to be done. There was no indication at the outset that this moment would behave differently than others.

He assessed. He prioritized. He acted.

The sequence held, at least at first.

But something in the situation resisted alignment. Not in a way that was immediately obvious. There was no single detail that signaled that things were off. It was more subtle than that—a sense that the pieces were not fitting together in the way they usually did, that the relationships between what was happening and what it meant were not resolving into something coherent.

He noticed it without naming it: a slight delay in clarity, a moment where the situation did not immediately organize itself into something that could be understood. He moved anyway. There was no time to wait for clarity. Action proceeded.

But the sense remained.

At first, he assumed it would resolve. It always had before. As more information became available, as the situation developed, as the sequence unfolded, things would come into focus. What seemed unclear would become clear. What seemed disjointed would come together. Meaning would stabilize.

But it didn't.

The more the situation progressed, the more it resisted that movement toward coherence. New information did not clarify—it complicated. Decisions did not resolve the tension—they exposed it. The structure that usually allowed him to understand what was happening did not fully hold.

He began to feel it more distinctly—not confusion, not exactly, but disorientation. It was the sense that something was not aligning, not just externally but internally. The way he was accustomed to making sense of things was not functioning in the same way. The connection between action and meaning, between event and understanding, was loosening.

He continued to act. He had to. The work did not pause because meaning was unclear.

But something had shifted.

He found himself reaching for explanation in the same way he always had. He tried to organize what was happening, to place it within the frameworks that had always worked. He traced cause and effect. He considered responsibility. He looked for patterns that would allow the situation to make sense.

But each explanation felt partial. It held one part of the experience, not the whole.

He could explain what had happened.

He could not fully explain what it meant.

This was new. Not the presence of uncertainty—he was familiar with that—but the absence of resolution, the inability to bring the experience into coherence.

The situation eventually ended, as all situations do. The actions were completed. The immediate demands were met. The external sequence reached its conclusion.

But internally, something remained open.

He began to revisit the moment—not because he wanted to, but because it did not settle. He returned to the details, reconstructed the sequence, examined the decisions. Each time, he expected the same thing: that it would resolve, that the missing piece would become visible, that the explanation would become complete, that the sense of disorientation would give way to clarity.

But it didn't.

The more he revisited the moment, the more he recognized that the issue was not simply that something was unclear. It was that something did not fit—not within the frameworks he had relied on, not within the assumptions that had allowed him to make sense of his work.

He began to notice what he had not noticed before: that he had expected things to make sense—not always immediately, not without effort, but eventually. That expectation had been so constant that he had never questioned it. It had functioned beneath awareness.

Now it was visible—not because it had been named, but because it had been disrupted.

He began to feel the absence of something he had never consciously identified—the absence of coherence.

And in that absence, something else began to emerge. Not panic. Not even fear.

But a quiet instability.

If this does not make sense, what else doesn't?

The question did not arrive fully formed. It developed. He began to notice it extending beyond the moment itself. If one situation could resist explanation, could others? If one decision could not be fully understood, what did that mean for the decisions that had come before—or the ones that would come after?

The issue was no longer confined to the event. It was moving into how he understood the world—and himself within it.

He had not lost his ability to act.

He had lost, or at least begun to lose, something else: the assumption that action would eventually resolve into meaning, that what he did would make sense, that the world, even when difficult, would hold together.

Now that assumption had been interrupted—not completely, not permanently, but enough that it could no longer be taken for granted.

He found himself carrying a new awareness: that stability is not always as stable as it appears, that coherence is not guaranteed, that meaning does not always follow action in the way he had expected.

This awareness did not stop him from continuing. He still showed up, still responded, still did the work.

But something in how he carried it had changed.

There was a question now—not always present, not always loud, but there:

Will this make sense?

And beneath that:

What happens if it doesn't?

The moment had not only resisted explanation. It had revealed something deeper—that the need for things to make sense had been there all along. And when that need is disrupted, the disruption does not stay contained within the moment.

It begins to move—through interpretation, through expectation, through the very structure of how reality is understood.

And once that movement begins, it does not easily stop.

This disruption of meaning is not foreign to the Christian tradition. It echoes a pattern in which expectation and reality no longer align, where what was assumed to hold no longer holds. The movement from hope to crucifixion is not only a narrative arc—it is an exposure of the limits of human certainty about how meaning is supposed to unfold. What was anticipated does not occur. What unfolds does not immediately make sense. The result is not simply confusion, but a deeper destabilization of the structures through which reality had been understood.

In that sense, the collapse of certainty is not an exception to faithful experience, but part of it. The question is not only how meaning is restored, but how it is carried when it is not yet clear. The theological dimensions of this movement—particularly the tension between expectation, suffering, and the reformation of meaning—are explored more fully in Hosanna to Crucifixion. Here, the focus remains on how that disruption is lived, interpreted, and carried in real time.

PART 2—THE STRUCTURE OF CERTAINTY AND THE LIMITS OF CONTROL

The experience described in the previous section is not unusual. It reflects a disruption of something that is often present but rarely examined: the expectation that experience will resolve into meaning. This expectation is not always explicit. It does not necessarily appear as a demand for certainty in every moment. Rather, it operates as an underlying assumption that, over time, what happens can be understood, integrated, and placed within a coherent framework.

This assumption functions as a stabilizing structure. It allows individuals to move through complex and demanding environments without becoming disoriented. Even when outcomes are uncertain and situations are unpredictable, there remains a sense that events can be interpreted in a way that makes them intelligible. This intelligibility is not the same as control over outcomes. It is control over meaning.

Control, in this sense, is often misunderstood. It is not primarily about determining what happens. It is about maintaining a sense that what happens can be understood.

This distinction is critical.

A person may operate effectively in highly unpredictable environments while still relying on a strong sense of interpretive stability. They may expect that, even if events do not unfold as planned, those events will eventually fit within a structure that explains them. Cause and effect will align. Responsibility will be identifiable. Outcomes will be interpretable.

When this expectation holds, it creates a form of psychological stability. The individual may experience difficulty, stress, or loss, but these experiences remain within a system that can absorb them. They can be explained, processed, and integrated into an ongoing understanding of the world.

Certainty, in this context, is not absolute. It is functional. It does not eliminate ambiguity; it contains it.

The difficulty arises when this structure does not hold. When an event resists interpretation, the issue is not simply that something is unclear. It is that the system through which clarity is normally achieved has been disrupted. The individual is no longer able to bring the experience into alignment with existing frameworks of meaning.

This is what creates disorientation.

The disruption is not only cognitive. It is structural.

To understand this more precisely, it is helpful to examine three interrelated elements: predictability, control, and coherence.

Predictability refers to the expectation that events will follow recognizable patterns. It does not require that outcomes be known in advance, but it assumes that there is a relationship between cause and effect that can be traced. When predictability is present, individuals can anticipate how situations are likely to unfold and adjust their actions accordingly.

Control refers to the perceived ability to influence outcomes. This includes both direct control—what a person can do—and indirect control—how a person interprets what they cannot influence. Even when direct control is limited, the ability to interpret events provides a sense of stability.

Coherence refers to the integration of experience into a meaningful whole. It is the sense that events, actions, and outcomes fit together in a way that can be understood. Coherence does not require that everything be resolved immediately. It requires that resolution remains possible.

These elements function together. Predictability supports control. Control supports coherence. Coherence reinforces the expectation of predictability.

When this system is intact, individuals are able to engage complex situations without losing their orientation. They may encounter uncertainty, but they do not lose their sense that uncertainty can be navigated.

When the system is disrupted, the effects extend across all three elements. Predictability breaks down as events no longer follow recognizable patterns. Control diminishes as the individual is unable to influence or interpret what is occurring. Coherence collapses as the experience resists integration into a meaningful whole.

This collapse does not always appear dramatically. It may emerge gradually. An individual may begin to notice that explanations feel incomplete, that cause and effect no longer align in expected ways, that responsibility cannot be clearly assigned, and that outcomes do not correspond to actions in predictable ways.

These observations may remain subtle at first. They may be dismissed or minimized. But over time, they accumulate.

And as they accumulate, they begin to challenge the underlying assumption that experience will resolve into meaning.

This is where distortion can begin to develop.

Distortion does not arise from a lack of intelligence or awareness. It arises from the need to restore stability.

When the system of predictability, control, and coherence is disrupted, the individual may attempt to reconstruct it in ways that are not fully accurate but feel more stable. A person may impose certainty where it does not exist, adopting rigid interpretations that reduce ambiguity but oversimplify the experience. They may assign responsibility in ways that are disproportionate, either over-attributing fault to themselves or externalizing it entirely. They may reinterpret events to fit within existing frameworks, even when those frameworks no longer fully hold.

These distortions are not failures. They are attempts at repair. The individual is trying to restore a sense of coherence, to bring the experience back into alignment with a system that can hold it.

However, when distortion becomes the primary means of maintaining stability, it can limit the ability to engage the experience accurately. The person may feel more certain, but that certainty is fragile. It depends on maintaining interpretations that may not fully account for the complexity of what occurred.

This is particularly significant in contexts where theological or moral frameworks are involved. Belief systems often provide powerful structures of meaning. They offer explanations for suffering, responsibility, and outcome. They provide language that can stabilize experience and support integration.

But when an event resists those frameworks, the individual may experience not only psychological disruption, but theological disruption.

Questions may arise that do not have immediate or clear answers: Why did this happen? What does this mean? Where was meaning in this?

If the existing framework cannot absorb these questions, the individual may attempt to resolve them prematurely. They may adopt explanations that restore certainty but do not fully engage the experience. They may reinforce beliefs in ways that protect stability but limit openness to complexity.

Again, these responses are not failures. They are efforts to maintain coherence.

The challenge is that premature certainty can prevent deeper engagement.

When certainty is imposed too quickly, it can close down the very process through which meaning might eventually be reformed.

The alternative is not the abandonment of structure. It is the capacity to remain within uncertainty without disengaging from it.

This requires a different kind of stability.

Not the stability of fixed explanation.

But the stability of sustained engagement.

To remain with an experience that does not yet make sense. To allow interpretation to develop over time. To resist the impulse to resolve complexity prematurely.

This is not passive.

It is active.

It involves holding tension without collapsing it. It involves recognizing that the absence of immediate coherence does not mean the absence of meaning. It involves acknowledging that the structures through which meaning is formed may themselves need to be examined, expanded, or reconfigured.

Certainty, control, and coherence are not inherently problematic. They are necessary. But when they are assumed to be guaranteed, their disruption can be destabilizing. When they are understood as provisional, their disruption can become part of a larger process of engagement.

This distinction is essential.

Because the goal is not to eliminate uncertainty.

It is to engage it without losing the capacity to act, to reflect, and to remain present within what has not yet been resolved.

PART 3—WHEN CERTAINTY COLLAPSES

The situation did not begin as a crisis of meaning. It began as a situation to be managed. There were variables to assess, decisions to make, and actions to carry out. He entered it the way he always did—attentive to what was in front of him, oriented toward response, grounded in the expectation that even complex situations would eventually resolve into something that could be understood.

At first, that expectation held. He could identify the elements of the situation. He could trace the relationships between them. He could determine what required immediate attention and what could wait. The structure of his thinking aligned with the structure of the moment. There was difficulty, but not disorientation. This is how certainty often operates—not as complete knowledge, but as functional alignment.

Then something shifted.

It did not occur all at once. There was no single point at which the situation became incomprehensible. Instead, small inconsistencies began to appear—information that did not align with what had already been understood, outcomes that did not follow from the actions that had been taken, responses that did not produce the expected results.

At first, these inconsistencies were manageable. He adjusted. He reconsidered. He reinterpreted what was happening, incorporating the new information into his understanding. This is how the system is meant to function. It adapts. It absorbs variation. It maintains coherence by adjusting interpretation. For a time, this process continued to work.

Then the inconsistencies accumulated, and the adjustments no longer resolved them.

Each attempt to restore alignment produced further misalignment. The more he tried to bring the situation into coherence, the more it resisted that movement. The relationships between action and outcome became increasingly unclear. Cause and effect no longer followed the patterns he expected.

This is the point at which certainty begins to weaken—not because the individual lacks ability, but because the structure through which ability operates is no longer sufficient.

He continued to act. He had to. The demands of the situation did not pause to allow for reorientation. Decisions still needed to be made. Actions still needed to be taken. The external sequence continued, even as the internal framework began to strain.

This created a divergence.

Outwardly, he was functioning.

Inwardly, something was becoming unstable.

He noticed it first as a delay—a moment longer to decide, a second consideration that had not been necessary before, a brief hesitation where there had once been immediacy. These were not failures. They were signals—signals that the alignment between perception and understanding was beginning to loosen.

He responded the way he always had. He sought clarity.

He attempted to reconstruct the situation in a way that made sense. He revisited the information, reassessed the priorities, reconsidered the sequence of actions. He worked to bring the experience back into a framework that could hold it.

But the framework did not fully respond.

It held parts of the experience.

Not the whole.

He could explain individual elements.

He could not integrate them.

This is where the collapse begins—not as a dramatic breakdown, but as a gradual loss of coherence. The situation no longer fits within the structures that have previously allowed it to be understood.

At this point, several responses become possible.

One is to narrow interpretation. He could focus on a single explanation and hold it tightly. He could simplify the situation, reduce its complexity, and impose a form of certainty that allowed him to continue acting without disruption. This would restore a degree of stability—but at a cost. The complexity of the situation would remain unaddressed.

Another response is to expand interpretation indefinitely. He could continue to search for explanations, adding layer upon layer of analysis in an attempt to account for every inconsistency. This would preserve the integrity of the experience, but it could also prevent resolution, leaving him in a state of ongoing uncertainty.

Neither response fully resolves the tension. Both represent attempts to manage the collapse.

In this case, he moved between them—at times simplifying, at times expanding. Neither held. The situation continued to resist full integration.

This resistance did something more than create difficulty.

It exposed an assumption.

That things should make sense.

Not immediately. Not easily.

But eventually.

This assumption had not been visible before because it had not been challenged. Now it was. And in being challenged, it revealed its importance.

He began to recognize that his ability to function had always been supported by the expectation of eventual coherence—that even when situations were complex, he believed they would resolve into something that could be understood.

Now that expectation was no longer holding.

The question was no longer simply, What is happening?

It became, What if this does not resolve?

This question introduced a different kind of instability—not about the situation alone, but about the structure through which the situation was being understood.

He continued to act. The work required it.

But the experience of acting had changed.

Each decision now carried an additional layer—not only what should be done, but will this make sense, and beneath that, what if it doesn't?

This is where certainty collapses into something else—not confusion, but exposure.

The realization that the systems of predictability, control, and coherence are not guaranteed. That they function most of the time, but not always. And when they do not, the individual is left without the structure that has previously supported their understanding.

This does not eliminate the ability to act.

But it changes how action is experienced.

He began to feel the difference—a subtle shift in how decisions were carried, a quiet awareness that resolution might not follow, a recognition that meaning might not emerge in the way he had expected.

This awareness did not paralyze him.

But it altered the ground beneath him.

The situation eventually ended. The external sequence concluded.

But the internal process did not.

He returned to the moment—not to re-decide, but to understand. And each time he returned, the same tension remained. The actions could be traced. The decisions could be explained.

But the meaning did not fully resolve.

This is the point at which certainty gives way to something else—not the absence of meaning, but the recognition that meaning is not always immediately accessible. That it may need to be held rather than solved, and that holding requires a different kind of stability.

One that does not depend on immediate coherence, but on the capacity to remain engaged—even when coherence is not yet available.

PART 4—REMAINING PRESENT WHEN MEANING DOES NOT RESOLVE

When certainty begins to loosen, the immediate impulse is to restore it. This impulse is not irrational. It reflects a need for stability that allows a person to continue functioning. When the structures of predictability, control, and coherence begin to strain, the individual looks for ways to bring the experience back into alignment. They seek explanation, resolution, or clarity—anything that can reestablish a sense that what is happening can be understood.

This movement toward resolution is natural. It is also, at times, premature.

The difficulty is not in the desire for certainty. It is in the timing.

When an experience has not yet settled, attempts to force it into resolution can limit the depth of engagement. The individual may adopt explanations that provide immediate relief but do not fully account for the complexity of what has occurred. They may simplify the situation, assign responsibility in ways that feel stable, or draw conclusions that close the experience before it has been fully examined.

These responses are understandable. They are efforts to restore coherence.

But they can also interrupt the process through which coherence might eventually emerge.

The alternative is not to abandon structure. It is to remain present within uncertainty.

Remaining present does not mean disengaging from the experience. It means staying in relationship to it without requiring that it resolve immediately.

This requires a different orientation.

Rather than asking, How do I make this make sense, the question becomes, How do I remain with this while it does not yet make sense?

This shift is subtle, but it is significant. It moves the focus from resolution to engagement.

To remain present in this way, several capacities become important.

The first is recognition. The individual must be able to identify when certainty is being imposed prematurely. This may appear as a sudden clarity that feels more relieving than accurate, an explanation that resolves tension quickly but leaves something unaddressed, or a conclusion that closes the experience without fully engaging it. Recognition allows the person to pause—not to stop thinking, but to reconsider the movement toward closure.

The second capacity is tolerance. In this context, tolerance refers to the ability to hold tension without immediately resolving it. This is not passive endurance. It is an active willingness to remain with an experience that is incomplete. It may involve sitting with questions that do not yet have answers, allowing multiple interpretations to coexist, and recognizing that uncertainty is not the same as failure. Tolerance creates space; without it, the individual is driven toward premature certainty.

The third capacity is differentiation. As uncertainty is held, it becomes important to distinguish between different elements of the experience. Not everything is equally unclear. Some aspects may be well understood, while others remain unresolved. Differentiation allows the individual to say, This part makes sense; this part does not. This prevents the experience from becoming globally destabilizing and allows uncertainty to be located rather than generalized.

The fourth capacity is continuity. The individual must be able to continue acting even when meaning is incomplete. This does not mean ignoring uncertainty. It means carrying it while remaining engaged in the work. Continuity is essential in environments where decisions cannot be delayed indefinitely. The person must act without full resolution, trusting that action and interpretation can continue to develop together. This is not comfortable, but it is necessary.

The fifth capacity is revision. As new understanding emerges, the individual must be willing to revisit previous interpretations. This involves flexibility—not in abandoning meaning, but in allowing meaning to develop over time. Revision acknowledges that understanding is not fixed; it is formed.

These capacities do not eliminate uncertainty. They make it inhabitable.

To hold uncertainty in this way is to resist two common extremes. One is premature closure—the insistence that the experience must be resolved now, that meaning must be fixed, that uncertainty is unacceptable. The other is disengagement—the withdrawal from the experience altogether, the decision not to engage what does not make sense.

Both responses reduce tension, but they do so by limiting engagement.

The middle space is more demanding. It requires staying present without forcing resolution, remaining engaged without collapsing into certainty, and continuing to act without full coherence.

This is the space in which deeper understanding becomes possible—not immediate understanding, but eventual integration.

Over time, experiences that initially resist meaning may begin to take shape. Not always in the form of clear answers, but in the form of a more developed understanding of what occurred and what it means. This process cannot be forced, but it can be supported.

The individual can return to the experience not to resolve it quickly, but to engage it more fully. They can allow interpretation to develop, response to be recognized, and meaning to emerge gradually.

This is a different kind of stability.

Not the stability of certainty.

But the stability of presence.

It is the ability to remain with what is not yet resolved without losing the capacity to act, to reflect, and to continue.

This kind of stability does not depend on everything making sense. It depends on the ability to remain engaged when it does not.

In this way, uncertainty becomes not only something to be managed, but something to be worked within. It becomes part of the process rather than a disruption of it. And through that process, meaning—though delayed—may begin to form in ways that are more accurate, more durable, and more deeply integrated than the certainty that was initially sought.

REFLECTION

When you encounter a moment that does not resolve, what is your first impulse?

Is it to explain it, resolve it, move past it, or stay with it?

Where do you notice yourself moving toward premature certainty?

Where do you find yourself withdrawing from what does not make sense?

What would it look like to remain present—to continue engaging—without requiring immediate resolution?

LOOKING AHEAD

We have seen how the expectation of control shapes moral experience.

Next, we will move into specific pathways in depth—beginning with the experience of perpetration.

SECTION II

Pathways and Processes

Chapter 6

Perpetration

PART 1—THE MOMENT THAT CROSSES THE LINE

He did not think of himself as someone who would do that.

If asked, he would have said there were lines he would not cross. Not in a rigid or abstract way, but in a way that had been formed over time. There were things he believed about himself—about what he would do, about what he would not do, about the kind of person he was within the work. These were not declarations he carried consciously. They were assumptions, built quietly, reinforced through repetition, confirmed in moments where decision and identity aligned.

He had acted before. He had made difficult decisions. He had done what was required, even when it carried cost. But those decisions had always remained within something he could recognize, within something he could carry. This felt different.

It did not begin as a violation. It began as a situation. There were competing demands, limited time, and no clear resolution that satisfied every need. The situation presented itself with the same familiar pressure—the sense that something had to be done, that delay would carry consequence, that inaction was not neutral.

He moved into it the way he always had. He assessed. He prioritized. He acted. At the time, the decision did not feel like crossing a line. It felt like choosing within constraint. There was no pause that allowed him to step outside of the moment and evaluate it from a distance. There was no space to ask whether the decision aligned fully with what he believed about himself. There was only the immediate need to respond, shaped by the conditions that were present.

He chose. The action followed. It was done.

From the outside, it appeared no different from other decisions. The situation moved forward. The immediate need was addressed. The sequence continued. Nothing stopped, and nothing announced that something had changed. But something had.

It did not show itself immediately. At first, there was only continuation—the next task, the next demand, the next decision. The rhythm of the work resumed, and he moved within it as he always had. If there was any sense that something had shifted, it remained beneath the surface, unformed and not yet recognizable.

Then, gradually, it returned.

Not as a full memory. Not as a replay. But as a recognition—a moment in which the action he had taken came back into view, not in its urgency or its necessity, but in its meaning. He saw it differently, not as what had needed to be done, but as what had been done. The distinction was small, but it mattered.

At the time, the decision had been shaped by pressure, by constraint, by the structure of the situation. It had felt justified within that context. It had felt necessary. Now, removed from that moment, the action stood on its own. In standing on its own, it became visible in a different way.

He began to feel it—not immediately as guilt, but as something quieter. A discomfort that did not attach itself to any specific thought, a sense that something did not align. He did not know what to do with it, so he did what he had learned to do. He explained it.

He returned to the situation, reconstructed the conditions, revisited the constraints. He traced the sequence again, placing the decision back into the context in which it had been made. It made sense there. It still made sense. But the sense did not hold in the same way, because the context was no longer present.

What remained was the action.

And the action did not fully resolve.

He noticed the difference. Other decisions, even difficult ones, could be placed back into their context and remain stable. They held together. They could be understood as part of the work, part of what had been required, part of what had been carried. This one did not settle in the same way.

It remained.

He began to return to it more often—not intentionally, but because it surfaced. In moments of stillness, in pauses between tasks, in the absence of immediate demand, it came back. It did not overwhelm. It did not disrupt his ability to function. But it persisted.

He began to ask the question, not out loud and not even fully formed.

Was that right?

The question did not accuse. It did not arrive with force. It remained open. He responded the way he knew how. Yes. It was what needed to be done. It followed from the situation. It aligned with the constraints.

The answer held.

But not completely.

Because another awareness had begun to form—that what had been necessary did not fully align with what he believed about himself. This was not immediately clear. It emerged slowly.

He began to notice the gap between action and identity—not a dramatic rupture, not a complete contradiction, but a misalignment. Something he had done did not fully fit within the person he understood himself to be.

This realization did not arrive all at once. It developed. At first, it appeared as hesitation when the moment returned, a slight resistance to revisiting it, a tendency to move past it quickly. But the moment did not disappear.

It stayed.

And in staying, it began to take shape.

He began to see not only the action, but what the action represented—a decision made under pressure, a choice that had consequences, a moment in which what was done could not be entirely reconciled with what he believed.

This was not a failure in the sense he was used to. It was not a mistake that could be corrected. It was not an outcome that could be revised.

It had already happened.

And it remained.

He began to feel the weight of that—not as punishment, but as presence. The action had entered into how he understood himself, not completely and not definitively, but enough that it could not be ignored.

He began to carry it—not constantly and not in every moment, but in a way that returned. The question deepened, not only Was that right, but What does that mean about me?

The shift was subtle, but it marked something important.

The moment was no longer only about what had been done. It had begun to move into identity. And once it moved there, it did not remain confined to the past. It began to shape how he approached the present.

Future decisions carried a different weight—not because he had lost his ability to act, but because he had become aware that action could cross a line he had not fully seen before. This awareness did not stop him, but it stayed with him.

The moment had not only been an event.

It had become a reference point—a place to which he returned, not to change it, but because it had changed something in him.

And in that change, something else had begun.

Not resolution.

But recognition—that it is possible to act in a way that does not fully align with who one believes oneself to be, and to carry that action forward not as something that disappears, but as something that remains.

PART 2—GUILT, AGENCY, AND RESPONSIBILITY

The experience described in the previous section centers on a particular kind of moral event: an action taken by the individual that does not fully align with their own values. This is distinct from situations in which harm is observed, imposed by others, or emerges through systemic failure. In this case, the individual is not only present within the event—they are an active participant in what has occurred. This introduces a different structure of moral experience in which the question is no longer only what happened, but what I did.

This shift places agency at the center.

Agency refers to the individual's capacity to act within a given situation. It includes both what was possible and what was chosen. In most circumstances, agency is experienced as constrained. Decisions are made under conditions of time pressure, limited information, competing demands, and incomplete control over outcomes. These constraints do not eliminate agency, but they shape how it is exercised. In situations of perpetration, agency is not absent—it is implicated.

The individual recognizes that the action that occurred cannot be attributed entirely to external forces. Even when the conditions were limiting, even when the decision felt necessary, there remains an awareness that the action was taken by them. This awareness is what gives rise to guilt.

Guilt, in this context, is not simply an emotional reaction. It is a moral recognition. It reflects the individual's perception that an action they took does not fully align with their internal framework of right and wrong. This recognition may be immediate, or it may develop over time as the individual revisits the moment outside the conditions in which it occurred. Guilt signals that something has not resolved.

It is important to distinguish this form of guilt from related experiences.

One distinction is between guilt and shame. Guilt is oriented toward action—what I did. Shame is oriented toward identity—what I am. While these experiences may become intertwined, they are not the same. Guilt identifies a discrepancy between action and value. Shame extends that discrepancy into a broader conclusion about the self. Maintaining this distinction is critical.

Another distinction is between guilt and regret. Regret reflects a desire that something had been different and may or may not involve moral judgment. Guilt, by contrast, carries an implicit evaluation: the action is experienced as morally significant, not merely unfortunate.

A further distinction is between guilt and responsibility. Responsibility refers to the role the individual had within the situation. It includes what they were accountable for, both formally and internally. Guilt arises when responsibility intersects with moral evaluation. These distinctions matter because they shape how the experience is understood and carried.

In situations of perpetration, responsibility is rarely simple.

The individual may have acted within a system that required certain responses. They may have been operating under constraints that limited their options. They may have been responding to competing obligations that could not all be fulfilled. This creates a layered structure of responsibility that includes what was required, what was possible, and what was chosen.

These layers do not always align.

An action may have been required within the system. It may have been the only viable option given the constraints. And yet, it may still conflict with the individual's values. This is where the experience becomes complex.

The presence of constraint does not eliminate the sense of agency, and the presence of agency does not eliminate the impact of constraint. The individual is left holding both: I had to act, and I did act. This dual awareness is what gives guilt its particular weight in situations of perpetration.

It is not simply that harm occurred.

It is that harm is connected to one's own action.

This connection does not need to be absolute to be significant. The individual may recognize that they were one factor among many. They may understand that the outcome cannot be attributed solely to their decision. They may be able to identify external pressures that shaped what occurred.

And yet, the action remains.

This is where attempts to resolve guilt often encounter difficulty.

One common response is to minimize agency. The individual may focus exclusively on the constraints of the situation, emphasizing what was not possible, what could not have been done differently, and what was required by circumstance. This can reduce the intensity of guilt, but it may also prevent the individual from fully engaging the moral dimension of the action.

Another response is to maximize agency. The individual may take on a disproportionate level of responsibility, interpreting the action as a reflection of personal failure. This can intensify guilt, sometimes to the point where it shifts into shame.

Both responses attempt to simplify a complex reality. One reduces responsibility; the other expands it beyond its actual scope. Neither fully accounts for the layered nature of agency within constrained conditions.

A more accurate understanding requires holding both elements together.

The individual acted within constraint.

And the action was theirs.

This does not resolve the tension.

It clarifies it.

Guilt, in this sense, is not a problem to be eliminated.

It is a signal to be understood.

It indicates that the individual's moral framework has been engaged, that there is a perceived discrepancy between action and value, and that this discrepancy has not yet been integrated. The goal, therefore, is not to remove guilt entirely, but to engage it in a way that allows for accurate understanding.

This involves examining the dimensions through which the experience is being carried.

At the level of meaning, the individual may need to consider what made the action significant—what, in that moment, carried moral weight. At the level of obligation, they may need to revisit what they believed they were responsible for and how those responsibilities were prioritized. At the level of judgment, they may need to explore how they are evaluating the action and whether that evaluation accounts for the full context. At the level of agency, they may need to examine what was actually possible, not only in retrospect but within the conditions that existed at the time. At the level of legacy, they may need to consider how the action is being integrated into their sense of self.

These dimensions do not eliminate guilt.

They give it structure.

Without this structure, guilt can become diffuse, expanding beyond the action into a broader sense of self-condemnation or, conversely, being suppressed in a way that prevents engagement. With structure, guilt can be located, understood in relation to specific aspects of the experience, and carried with greater precision.

And in that precision, the possibility of constructive engagement begins.

PART 3—WHEN ACTION CONFLICTS WITH IDENTITY

The moment did not present itself as a violation at the time. It presented as a decision. There were competing demands, limited time, and no option that resolved every need. He moved into the situation with the same orientation he had relied on before—attentive to what was in front of him, oriented toward response, grounded in the expectation that a course of action could be identified and carried forward.

At first, the structure held. He assessed what was in front of him. He identified the elements that required attention. He began to prioritize. The sequence was familiar, shaped by repetition and reinforced through experience. It did not require extended reflection. It unfolded as a practiced response. Under ordinary conditions, this process produces clarity.

In this moment, it did not fully resolve.

Two obligations emerged, both carrying weight and both requiring response. At the level of meaning, each appeared significant. Neither could be dismissed as secondary. One involved immediate need, visible and pressing. The other involved consequence that was less immediate but no less real. The framework through which he usually organized significance did not provide a clear hierarchy.

He still had to act, but the action did not emerge from clear ordering. It emerged from constraint.

At the level of obligation, the tension intensified. He was responsible for responding to what was in front of him. He was responsible for acting within the expectations of his role. He was responsible for outcomes that extended beyond the immediate moment. These responsibilities did not align. To fulfill one required the partial neglect of another.

This is where the decision took shape—not as a clear affirmation of one value over another, but as a movement in one direction under pressure.

He chose.

The action followed.

At the time, the decision could be justified. It aligned with one set of obligations. It followed a recognizable pattern. It could be explained within the structure of the situation. He continued, and the moment did not stop.

But later, when the situation had passed and the immediate demands had receded, the decision returned—not as a problem to solve, but as something to be understood.

He began to revisit it. At first, he reconstructed the sequence. He examined the conditions. He reviewed the constraints. Within that reconstruction, the decision still made sense. It held.

But something else had begun to emerge.

The sense that the decision, while understandable, did not fully align with how he understood himself.

This is where the conflict becomes visible—not between two external options, but between action and identity.

He began to examine the decision through a different lens. Not only what happened, but what does this say about me. This shift altered the structure of the experience.

At the level of judgment, the decision became more complex. It could still be defended, but it could not be fully settled. There was no single evaluation that resolved the tension. Within one framework, the action was appropriate. Within another, it remained questionable. The coexistence of these evaluations created a form of moral ambiguity that did not collapse into a single conclusion.

At the level of agency, the moment remained constrained. He recognized the limits within which he had been operating. Time had been insufficient. Options had been limited. Information had been incomplete. These constraints shaped the decision in ways that could not be ignored.

But recognition of constraint did not eliminate the sense of authorship.

The action was still his.

This dual awareness remained: I could not do everything, and I did choose.

The tension between these two realities did not resolve. It deepened.

As the moment continued to return, he began to notice how it was being carried—not only as a memory, but as a reference point. Future decisions were not identical to this one, but they were no longer entirely separate from it.

He became more aware of the possibility that action could conflict with identity—not as a theoretical risk, but as something that had already occurred.

This awareness altered his orientation.

He began to approach situations with a different kind of attention—not only to what needed to be done, but to how what was done might later be understood. This did not produce clarity. It introduced caution.

At times, that caution was helpful. It slowed decision-making just enough to allow for greater awareness. At other times, it created hesitation. The concern was no longer only about outcome.

It was about alignment.

Would this fit with who I am?

And beneath that:

What if it doesn't?

This question did not prevent action, but it remained present.

The moment had moved beyond its original context. It had become part of how he interpreted himself within the work.

At the level of legacy, the impact became more visible. The decision had not defined him, but it had influenced how he understood his own capacity—not only the capacity to act well, but the capacity to act in ways that did not fully align with his values.

This recognition did not resolve into a single conclusion. It did not lead to a clear redefinition of identity.

It remained open.

He began to hold two realities simultaneously: I am someone who seeks to act in alignment with my values, and I am someone who has acted in ways that do not fully align.

These realities did not cancel each other out.

They coexisted.

The work, then, was not to eliminate one in favor of the other. It was to understand how both could be held—without collapsing into self-condemnation and without dismissing the significance of the action.

This is where the experience of perpetration becomes distinct. The tension is not only about what occurred. It is about how what occurred is integrated into identity.

The decision cannot be undone, but its meaning is not fixed.

It continues to develop through interpretation, through reflection, and through how the individual chooses to engage what remains.

The moment, then, is not only something that happened. It is something that continues—not in repetition of the action, but in the ongoing process of understanding what that action means and how it is carried forward.

PART 4—WORKING CONSTRUCTIVELY WITH GUILT

When an action remains, the impulse is often to resolve it quickly. The individual may seek to determine whether the decision was right or wrong, to reach a conclusion that settles the tension, or to find a way to move past the experience so that it no longer intrudes into the present. This movement toward resolution is understandable. It reflects a desire for coherence and for the restoration of alignment between action and identity.

But in situations of perpetration, resolution is rarely immediate.

The action has occurred. It cannot be undone. What remains is not the decision itself, but how the decision is being carried, and guilt is part of that carrying. The question is not how to eliminate guilt. It is how to engage it constructively.

The first step is recognition. Recognition involves acknowledging that guilt is present without immediately attempting to resolve it. This may take the form of simple language: this stayed with me; I continue to return to this moment; something about this does not settle. These statements do not analyze the experience. They locate it.

Recognition prevents two common responses.

One is suppression. The individual may attempt to move past the experience, minimizing its significance or avoiding it altogether. This can reduce immediate discomfort, but it often leaves the underlying tension unaddressed.

The other is escalation. The individual may expand the experience beyond its actual scope, allowing guilt to generalize into broader conclusions about the self. What began as a response to a specific action becomes a statement about identity.

Recognition interrupts both patterns. It allows the experience to be held in place long enough to be examined.

The second step is differentiation. Guilt often arrives as a single, undivided weight. Everything feels connected, and therefore everything feels equally significant. Differentiation involves separating the elements of the experience so that they can be understood more precisely.

This includes distinguishing between what was done, what was intended, what was possible, and what was required. These elements do not always align. An action may have produced an outcome that was not intended. An intention may have been shaped by constraints that limited what was possible. What was required may have conflicted with what was valued.

Without differentiation, these layers collapse into a single conclusion: I did something wrong.

With differentiation, the structure becomes more visible. This is what I did. This is what I intended. This is what was possible. This is what I was responding to.

This does not eliminate guilt.

It gives it shape.

The third step is locating responsibility accurately. As described earlier, responsibility in these moments is layered. There are elements of the situation that belong to the individual and elements that do not. Working constructively with guilt requires distinguishing between these.

This involves asking: what, in this situation, was mine to carry? What, in this situation, was not? These questions are not asked to reduce responsibility or to increase it. They are asked to locate it.

When responsibility is inaccurately expanded, guilt can become overwhelming. The individual may carry aspects of the situation that were never within their control. When responsibility is minimized, guilt may be dismissed in a way that prevents engagement.

Accurate location allows the experience to be engaged without distortion.

The fourth step is remaining in relationship to the action. There is a tendency to move quickly toward separation—to treat the action as something that no longer belongs to the self, something that can be set aside or dismissed. In some cases, this takes the form of justification. In others, it takes the form of avoidance.

Working constructively with guilt requires a different approach.

The action is acknowledged as part of one's history—not as a total definition of the self, but not as something external to it either. This creates a more complex relationship: I did this, and I am more than this. These statements are held together without collapsing one into the other.

The fifth step is allowing interpretation to develop over time. Guilt often carries an urgency—the sense that it must be resolved quickly, that a conclusion must be reached, that the experience must be settled. This urgency can lead to premature closure, where the individual adopts an explanation that provides relief but does not fully account for the complexity of the moment.

Allowing interpretation to develop means resisting that urgency. It involves returning to the experience gradually, examining it from different perspectives, and allowing understanding to form over time. This does not guarantee resolution, but it allows for a more accurate engagement.

The sixth step is recognizing the role of repair. Repair does not always take the form of direct correction. In some cases, the consequences of an action cannot be undone. But repair can still occur in how the individual responds moving forward.

This may involve changes in how decisions are made, increased attention to areas where misalignment occurred, or a re-examination of the values that guide action. Repair is not a reversal of the past. It is a response to it.

Importantly, repair does not eliminate guilt.

It changes how it is carried.

The individual is no longer only holding what was done. They are also engaged in what is being done in response. This introduces movement without requiring resolution.

Working constructively with guilt, then, is not a linear process. It does not move from guilt to its absence. It moves from undifferentiated weight to structured engagement, from immediate reaction to sustained reflection, and from isolation to integration.

The action remains.

The question is how it is carried.

When guilt is engaged in this way, it does not disappear. But it may become more precise, more contained, and more connected to specific aspects of the experience. This precision allows the individual to remain in relationship to the action without being defined entirely by it.

It allows the tension between action and identity to be held without collapsing into self-condemnation or dismissal.

And within that tension, something else becomes possible.

Not resolution in the sense of closure.

But a form of integration in which the action is neither denied nor allowed to define the whole.

It becomes part of the ongoing process of understanding what it means to act, to choose, and to carry those choices forward.

REFLECTION

When you return to a moment in which your own action remains unsettled, where does the weight of that experience feel most concentrated?

Is it in what was done, in what was intended, in what was possible, or in how the action is now being interpreted?

How are you locating responsibility within that moment?

Where might responsibility be expanded beyond what was yours to carry?

Where might it be minimized in ways that prevent engagement?

What would it look like to remain in relationship to the action without allowing it to define the whole of who you are?

LOOKING AHEAD

We have seen how moral injury can emerge through one's own actions.

Next, we will consider the experience of witnessing—what it means to carry what one has seen but not caused.

Chapter 7

Witnessing

PART 1—WHAT SHOULD NOT BE SEEN

He did not expect it to stay with him.

At the time, it was one moment among many. The day had already been full—decisions made, needs addressed, attention divided across more demands than could be fully held. Nothing about the moment announced itself as different. It did not arrive with clarity. It did not pause the sequence or interrupt the work. It appeared as other moments appeared, within the ongoing movement of responsibility.

It happened, and then the work continued.

He had seen difficult things before. This was not new. He had been present in situations where outcomes were uncertain, where people were in distress, where decisions carried weight that extended beyond the immediate moment. Over time, he had learned how to move through such environments without stopping, how to register what was happening without becoming fixed to it. The rhythm had become familiar—notice, respond, continue. It was not indifference. It was function. It allowed him to remain effective in situations that did not permit extended reflection.

This followed the same pattern, at first.

He saw what was happening. He understood enough to know that it mattered. He recognized, without needing to name it, that something was not right—that something was unfolding in a way that should not have been occurring. The recognition was present, but it did not interrupt the sequence.

There was no pause.

There was no intervention.

Not because he did not care, but because the moment did not allow for it. There were constraints—structural, relational, situational. The lines of authority were already drawn. The roles were already in place. The sequence had already begun to move, and there was no clear point at which he could enter it in a way that would alter its course without creating a different kind of disruption. The space in which action might have been taken was either too narrow or already passed by the time it could be recognized.

He registered it.

And then he continued.

From the outside, nothing remained. The situation moved forward. The moment was absorbed into the larger flow of the day. Other needs presented themselves. Other decisions required attention. The sequence continued without interruption, and there was no visible marker that distinguished this moment from any other.

It passed.

But it did not leave.

At first, it returned without form—not as a clear memory and not as a replay, but as an impression. A sense that something had been seen that did not settle, something that had not fully integrated into the ongoing movement of experience. It appeared briefly, then receded, as though it were no different from other difficult moments that had been encountered and absorbed over time.

He did not immediately attend to it. There were other things requiring attention. The rhythm of the work did not slow to allow for reflection. The next moment arrived, and then the next, and then the next. The structure of the day did not create space for returning to what had already passed.

The moment seemed to recede.

Until it returned again.

This time with more clarity.

He began to see it not as a passing occurrence, but as a moment that had not resolved. The details became more distinct. The sequence of what had happened became more defined. What had been only an impression began to take shape, and with that shape came a clearer awareness that something within the moment remained unsettled.

He began to ask himself what had actually happened—not in the sense of reconstructing the event, but in the sense of understanding its meaning.

He had seen something.

That much was clear.

But what he had seen did not fit easily into the categories he used to interpret his own actions. It was not a decision he had made. It was not an outcome he had directly caused. It was not something he could correct or change. It existed outside of the structures he relied on to make sense of his role.

And yet, it remained.

He began to feel the weight of that—not as responsibility in the way he understood responsibility for his own actions, but as something less defined and more difficult to locate. A sense that being present had not been neutral, that seeing what had happened had created a connection that did not dissolve when the moment passed.

He returned to the moment again, this time with a different question.

Should something have been done?

The question did not arrive with accusation. It did not demand an immediate answer. But it carried a different kind of tension, one that extended beyond what had occurred into what might have been possible.

He began to consider the conditions again—the constraints, the roles, the timing. He looked for the point at which action might have been taken, the moment at which intervention might have been possible. He examined the sequence as it had unfolded, searching for a place where the outcome could have been altered.

It was not clear.

There were reasons he had not acted. The boundaries of his role had been present. The limitations of the moment had been real.

And yet, the question remained.

He began to notice that the moment was changing in how it was being carried. It was no longer only about what had been seen. It was about what it meant to have seen it.

This shift altered the experience.

He was no longer only an observer.

He was implicated.

Not through action.

But through presence.

The recognition did not fade. It settled into a quiet awareness that something had occurred that should not have occurred, and that he had been there when it did.

He had seen it.

And in seeing it, something had been established—a connection that did not dissolve when the moment passed.

He began to notice how this awareness affected him afterward. Not in the moment, but when the pace slowed, when there was space to think, when the next demand had not yet arrived. The moment returned—not always fully, sometimes only as a fragment: a detail, a gesture, a tone that pointed back without reconstructing everything.

Each time, it carried the same quality.

It did not settle.

He began to understand that the difficulty was not only in what had occurred. It was in the fact that he had witnessed it—that he had been present, that he had seen something that should not have happened, and that there had been no clear way to respond within the moment itself.

This recognition did not resolve into a conclusion.

It remained open.

He began to carry the moment differently—not as something that had passed, but as something that continued.

It became a reference point.

Other moments passed.

This one stayed.

And in staying, it began to shape how he understood what it meant to be present within situations like this—not only what he did, but what he saw. He began to recognize that there are moments in which seeing is not neutral, in which presence itself creates a form of involvement that is not defined by action but is not separate from it either.

This realization did not resolve the tension.

It clarified it.

He had witnessed something.

And in witnessing it, he had become part of it in a way that could not be easily named.

The moment did not end when it passed.

It continued.

And in continuing, it began to ask something of him.

What does it mean to carry what has been seen?

The question remained.

PART 2—SECONDARY MORAL INJURY AND THE BURDEN OF SEEING

The experience described in the previous section centers on a form of moral engagement that does not arise from direct action, but from presence. The individual does not initiate the event, nor do they determine its outcome. Instead, they encounter a situation in which something occurs that conflicts with their moral framework, and they are positioned as a witness to that occurrence. This introduces a distinct pathway within moral injury in which the central question is no longer only what I did, but what I saw.

This shift alters the structure of the experience.

In situations of perpetration, the individual is directly connected to the action, and the moral tension emerges from the relationship between action and value. In situations of inaction, the individual is aware of a failure to act, and the tension arises from the gap between what was possible and what was done. In witnessing, the individual occupies a different position. They are neither the primary agent nor entirely removed. They are present within the situation, aware of what is occurring, but not fully able to determine how it unfolds.

Presence, in this context, is not neutral.

To witness an event is not simply to observe it in a detached sense. It is to register it within one's interpretive framework and carry that recognition forward. The act of witnessing establishes a connection between the event and the individual—not through authorship, but through exposure.

This is the basis of secondary moral injury.

Secondary moral injury refers to the moral impact of encountering actions, decisions, or outcomes that violate one's sense of what should occur, even when the individual is not directly responsible. It arises through exposure rather than authorship. The individual is not the source of the action, but they are not separate from its effects. The pathway is indirect, not diminished.

Because the individual did not act, this pathway is often less visible.

The absence of direct responsibility can obscure the presence of moral impact, allowing the experience to be treated as part of the environment rather than something carried.

And yet, the impact remains.

At the level of meaning, the individual recognizes that what has been witnessed carries moral weight. The event is not experienced as neutral or routine. It is interpreted as something that should not have occurred, or as something that conflicts with what the individual understands to be right. This recognition may be immediate or develop over time.

Meaning, in this context, is not assigned abstractly.

It is felt.

The individual does not need to articulate a formal judgment to recognize that something is wrong. The recognition often precedes language.

At the level of obligation, the experience becomes more complex. The individual may feel a sense of responsibility, but that responsibility is difficult to locate. They may not have had the authority to intervene, the capacity to alter the outcome, or the opportunity to act.

And yet, the recognition that something is wrong generates a sense that something should be done.

This is where moral distress begins to take shape.

Moral distress refers to recognizing what one believes to be the right course of action while being unable to carry it out. In witnessing, this takes the form of seeing something that should not occur and being unable to intervene.

I know this is not right.

And I cannot change it.

This dual awareness creates tension that does not resolve through action. It remains active because the recognition is intact while the capacity to respond is constrained.

At the level of judgment, the individual evaluates what has been seen. This evaluation may be directed toward the actions of others, the decisions made, or the outcomes that resulted. In some cases, the evaluation is clear. In others, it remains layered.

The individual may understand contributing factors while still experiencing the outcome as wrong.

This creates moral ambiguity.

Not uncertainty about whether something matters.

But about how to fully interpret it.

At the level of agency, the individual's capacity is constrained. They may return to the moment and consider what could have been done differently, examining the boundaries of their role, authority, and context.

This process does not always produce clarity.

In many cases, it reinforces the limits that were present.

And yet, the question persists.

Could something have been done?

This question does not necessarily lead to a definitive answer.

It remains active.

At the level of legacy, the impact of witnessing becomes more visible over time. The individual begins to integrate the experience into their understanding of themselves and their work through repeated exposure and reflection.

A single instance may not carry lasting weight.

But witnessing is rarely singular.

Over time, the individual encounters multiple moments that do not align with their moral framework and cannot be easily changed. Each may remain partially unresolved.

Together, they create a cumulative effect.

The individual is not only carrying one moment.

They are carrying many.

This accumulation shapes how the individual experiences their work. It may alter expectations, influence perception, and introduce a guarded awareness that presence does not guarantee influence.

This does not require disengagement.

But it changes how engagement is experienced.

The individual remains present, but with recognition of limits that cannot always be overcome.

This awareness can be difficult to hold.

It challenges assumptions about control, responsibility, and role.

It raises questions that do not easily resolve.

What is my responsibility when I witness something I cannot change?

What does it mean to remain present when outcomes do not align with what I believe is right?

How do I carry what I have seen?

These questions do not produce immediate answers.

They remain active within the experience.

Secondary moral injury, then, is not defined by a single event.

It is shaped by the interaction between exposure, interpretation, and unresolved tension. The individual does not move past the moment simply because it has ended.

They carry it.

And in carrying it, they continue to engage its meaning over time.

This engagement may not lead to resolution.

But it shapes how the experience is understood and carried forward.

PART 3—CARRYING WHAT WAS SEEN

The moment did not begin as something that required analysis. It unfolded in front of him, within a sequence that did not pause to allow for interpretation. He was present, positioned to see what was occurring, but not in a position to determine how it would unfold. The event moved forward according to a structure already in motion, shaped by decisions made before he entered it.

At the time, his role was clear enough. He was there to observe, to support where possible, to remain within established boundaries. The structure of the situation did not place him in primary authority. Decisions were being made by others, and actions were already underway. His presence did not include the ability to redirect the sequence without introducing consequences beyond the moment itself.

He registered what was happening.

He understood enough to recognize that something was not right.

But he did not act.

At the level of meaning, the moment carried immediate significance. What he saw did not align with what he believed should occur. The details may have been complex, but the sense of misalignment was not. Something had crossed a boundary—not necessarily a formal rule, but a moral expectation formed through experience and conviction.

At the level of obligation, the experience became more complicated. He was not responsible for directing the situation, nor positioned to override decisions already in motion. The roles were defined, and his role did not include intervention at that level.

And yet, the awareness of what was happening generated a sense of responsibility.

Not formal.

But internal.

He felt the tension between what he was assigned to do and what he believed should be done. The structure limited his ability to act, but not his awareness of the need for action.

This is where moral distress began to take shape.

He recognized what was right.

And could not carry it out.

The moment did not allow for resolution through action.

At the level of judgment, he evaluated what he had seen. This evaluation was not simple. There were elements that could be explained, contextual factors that shaped what occurred. The actions of others were not without reason, and the conditions were not entirely within their control.

He could see the structure.

He could understand the pressures.

And yet, the sense that something was wrong remained.

The evaluation did not collapse into a single conclusion. It remained layered. He could recognize complexity while still experiencing the outcome as misaligned with what should have occurred.

This created moral ambiguity.

Not uncertainty about whether something mattered.

But about how to fully interpret it.

At the level of agency, the constraints of the situation became more visible over time. He returned to the moment and examined what had been possible. He considered whether there had been a point where he could have intervened without creating additional harm or disruption.

The answers were not clear.

There were moments that appeared, in retrospect, to hold potential for action. But those moments were narrow, shaped by timing, authority, and context. Acting within them would have required stepping outside the role he had been given.

He recognized the limits.

And yet, the question remained.

Could something have been done?

This question did not resolve into certainty. It remained active—not as accusation, but as inquiry.

At the level of legacy, the experience began to shift. The moment was no longer only something that had occurred. It became something that was carried. The act of witnessing had created a connection that extended beyond the original context.

He began to notice how it affected him—not in a way that prevented him from continuing his work, but in a way that altered how he understood his presence within it.

He became more aware that what he might see would not always align with what he believed should happen. This did not remove him from the work, but it changed how he inhabited it. He remained engaged, with a clearer recognition that engagement does not guarantee influence.

The moment became a reference point—not because it was unique, but because it had not resolved.

It returned.

I saw this.

And I could not change it.

This did not accuse.

But it carried weight.

As similar moments accumulated, the pattern became more defined. He was not only carrying one instance of witnessing, but many. Each reinforced the awareness that recognition and action do not always align.

This accumulation intensified the experience.

Not through a single overwhelming event.

But through repetition.

The burden of witnessing became ongoing, present across situations rather than confined to one moment. It shaped how he understood the environment and his role within it.

He began to notice changes in how he responded. At times, a heightened awareness—a readiness to identify moments where intervention might be possible. At other times, a recognition of limitation—that not all situations could be altered.

These responses did not cancel each other out.

They coexisted.

The tension remained.

The experience of witnessing was not defined only by what had been seen, but by how it continued to be carried. Across the dimensions, a pattern emerged.

Meaning clear.

Obligation unresolved.

Judgment layered.

Agency constrained.

Legacy cumulative.

None of these dimensions resolved fully. They remained active, shaping the experience over time.

The moment did not settle because it could not be fully integrated through action, explanation, or immediate understanding.

It remained.

And in remaining, it continued to shape how he understood what it means to be present, to see, and to carry what cannot be easily changed.

PART 4—PROCESSING WHAT HAS BEEN SEEN

When a moment is witnessed and does not resolve, the impulse is often to move past it. The event has ended. The sequence has continued. Other demands have taken priority. In many environments, there is no natural pause that allows the individual to remain with what has occurred. The expectation—whether stated or implied—is that the work continues, and that what has been seen is absorbed into that continuation.

In some cases, this movement forward is necessary. The structure of the work requires it. The pace of the environment does not allow for extended reflection. Decisions must continue to be made, and attention must remain directed toward what is immediately in front of the individual.

But when a moment does not settle, moving past it does not mean it has been processed.

What remains is not only the memory of the event, but the experience of having witnessed it. The connection established through seeing does not dissolve simply because the moment has ended. It continues to exist within the individual's experience, returning in ways that are not always predictable.

The question, then, is not how to forget what has been seen.

It is how to engage it.

The first movement is recognition. Recognition involves acknowledging that a moment has not settled. This does not require full analysis. It begins with noticing that something remains active.

This recognition often takes simple form: I keep returning to that. Something about that did not sit right. I cannot fully explain it, but it remains.

Recognition interrupts two common distortions.

The first is dismissal. The individual may minimize the moment because they were not directly responsible. This can create distance but leaves the tension unaddressed.

The second is absorption. The individual may take the entire weight into themselves, internalizing what was seen as though it were their own action.

Recognition prevents both.

It allows the experience to be held without distortion.

The second movement is differentiation. In witnessing, there is a critical distinction between what was seen and what was done. The individual did not initiate the action. They did not determine the outcome.

And yet, they were present.

Differentiation involves holding this clearly: I saw this, and I did not do this. This does not remove the impact, but it locates it.

Without this distinction, the individual may carry responsibility that is not theirs or distance themselves in ways that prevent engagement.

The third movement is locating responsibility accurately. Responsibility in witnessing is often diffuse. There may be aspects that fall within the individual's role and aspects that do not.

Working constructively requires asking: what was mine to carry, and what was not?

These questions are not about blame.

They are about clarity.

Accurate location allows the individual to engage what belongs to them without taking on what does not.

The fourth movement is acknowledging limitation. One of the central tensions in witnessing is the gap between recognition and action. The individual sees something that should not occur, but cannot change it. This limitation may be structural, situational, or relational.

Acknowledging limitation does not resolve the tension.

It names it.

It allows the individual to say: I saw this, and I could not alter it within the conditions that were present.

This situates the experience within reality.

The fifth movement is allowing the experience to remain without forcing resolution. There is often an impulse to determine what should have been done. This can lead to repeated attempts to resolve a moment that cannot be undone.

Not all moments resolve.

Some remain open.

This does not indicate failure.

It reflects the limits of the situation.

The sixth movement is relational engagement. Witnessed moments are often carried in isolation. The individual may not have a context in which to speak about what was seen, or may assume that doing so is unnecessary.

And yet, speaking the experience changes how it is held.

Not by resolving it immediately, but by allowing it to be named and understood in relation to another.

The goal is not to determine whether the individual should have acted differently.

The goal is to understand how the experience is being carried.

Questions that support this include: What did you see? What remains with you? Where is the tension most present? What did you experience as possible in that moment?

These questions do not resolve the event.

They open it.

The seventh movement is recognizing accumulation. Witnessing is rarely a single event. Over time, the individual encounters multiple moments that do not align with their moral framework and cannot be easily changed.

Each may remain partially unresolved.

Together, they create a cumulative effect.

The individual is not only carrying one moment.

They are carrying many.

Recognizing this shifts the focus from a single event to a pattern. The weight being carried is not only from what happened once, but from what has been repeatedly seen and not fully integrated.

Processing witnessed injustice is not a movement toward elimination.

It is a movement toward clarity.

From dismissal or over-identification to accurate location.

From undifferentiated weight to structured understanding.

From isolation to relational engagement.

The moment remains.

But it can be carried differently.

Not as something that intrudes without form, but as something recognized, located, and engaged.

This does not remove the tension.

It allows the individual to remain in relationship to what has been seen without being overwhelmed by it.

And in that relationship, the experience takes on a different shape.

Not resolved.

But held.

REFLECTION

When you think back to moments you have witnessed that did not settle, what remains most clearly?

Is it the event itself, or the fact that you were there to see it?

What did you recognize in the moment that you could not act on?

Where do you find yourself still holding that recognition?

How do you understand your role in what you witnessed—not in terms of blame, but in terms of presence?

Where might you be carrying responsibility that was never yours?

Where might you be minimizing what you saw because you did not act?

What happens when you allow both to be held accurately?

When you return to those moments, what feels unresolved?

Is it the outcome, the lack of intervention, or the question of what might have been possible?

How do you relate to the limits that were present in that moment?

What would it mean to acknowledge those limits without dismissing what you recognized?

As you consider the accumulation of what you have witnessed, what pattern begins to emerge?

What has repeated?

What has remained unfinished?

How has this shaped how you see your work, your role, and your expectations of what can be changed?

What does it look like to carry what you have seen without becoming either detached or overwhelmed?

What would it mean to remain present to what you have witnessed without requiring it to resolve?

WHAT'S AHEAD

We have seen that witnessing carries its own moral weight.

Next, we will turn to the experience of inaction—what happens when one could not or did not act.

Chapter 8

Failure to Act

PART 1—THE MOMENT OF HESITATION

IT DID NOT BEGIN with a decision.

It began with a pause.

Not a long pause. Not something visible to anyone else. There was no interruption in the flow of the moment, no outward sign that anything had shifted. The sequence continued as it always did—voices moving, actions unfolding, attention directed toward what seemed most immediate. But within that movement, something slowed.

He noticed it without naming it. A sense that something was happening that required response. Not dramatic. Not urgent in a way that demanded immediate action. But present enough to register, to create a slight separation between what was unfolding and how he was experiencing it.

There was a moment.

And within that moment, there was a question.

He did not frame it clearly at the time. It did not arrive as language. It arrived as tension—a recognition that something could be done, or should be done, without clarity about what that action would look like or what it would require.

The moment did not stop to allow him to decide. It moved, and he moved with it.

There were reasons. There are always reasons. The situation was complex. Other priorities pressed in. The outcome was not yet certain. The cost of stepping in was not fully known. There were roles to consider, boundaries that had been established, expectations that shaped what was appropriate within the moment. Acting would have meant stepping into something not yet defined.

So he waited.

Not indefinitely. Just long enough. Long enough for the moment to pass from possibility into outcome.

By the time he recognized that the opportunity had closed, there was nothing left to act on. The moment had moved, and he had moved with it.

From the outside, nothing appeared wrong. The situation continued. The sequence resolved into what it would become. There was no visible marker of what had been possible, no external indication that anything had been missed.

But something remained.

At first, it did not present itself as regret. It was quieter than that—a sense that something had been left undone. Not in the sense of failure as it is typically understood—no clear mistake, no identifiable error—but in the sense that a possibility had been present and had not been taken.

He returned to the moment. Not immediately, not all at once, but in fragments—details, phrases, shifts in tone. Each return carried the same underlying question, though it had not yet taken full form.

What happened there?

He replayed the sequence, not to reconstruct it perfectly, but to understand where the opening had been. He looked for the point at which action might have been possible, the moment where something different could have occurred.

It became clearer over time.

There had been a space—small, brief, but real. A point at which he could have stepped in, said something, altered the direction of what was unfolding. It would not have required certainty. It would not have required control. It would have required movement—an interruption, a decision to act before all the variables were known.

He had not moved.

At the time, the reasons made sense. They still made sense. The uncertainty had been real. The potential consequences had been unclear. The boundaries had been present. The moment had not demanded action in a way that removed all ambiguity.

And yet, something in him recognized that those reasons were not the whole story.

There had also been hesitation—not fear in its most obvious form, but something quieter. A reluctance to step into a moment not fully defined. A preference for clarity the situation did not provide. A waiting for the moment to declare itself before committing to action.

The moment did not declare itself.

It passed.

And what remained was not only what had happened, but what had not.

He felt the shift from observation to implication. This was not something he had witnessed. It was something he had been part of—not through action, but through inaction.

The distinction mattered.

He had not caused the outcome. But he had not interrupted it. And that difference did not remove him from the moment. It placed him within it.

He returned again, this time with a different clarity.

I should have said something.

The sentence did not arrive all at once. It formed gradually, as the fragments of the moment aligned into a clearer understanding of what had been possible. It was not an accusation. It was not yet fully regret.

It was recognition.

There had been a moment. He had been in it. And he had not acted.

The sentence repeated, not as a loop, but as a reference point.

I should have said something.

He tested it against the conditions of the moment. He revisited the constraints, the uncertainty, the lack of clarity. He examined the reasons again—not to dismiss them, but to see whether they held.

They did.

And still, the sentence remained.

I should have said something.

It began to take on weight—not because it was dramatic, but because it was persistent. It did not resolve. It did not fade. It stayed present, shaping how he understood the moment each time he returned to it.

He noticed how it extended beyond that single instance. Other moments came into view—different situations, different contexts, but the same structure: recognition, pause, decision not to act, and afterward, the same sentence.

I should have. . .

The specifics changed.

The pattern did not.

He understood that the difficulty was not only in what had been missed, but in how the moment had been lived. The hesitation was not an isolated event. It was part of a way of moving through uncertainty—waiting for clarity, delaying action until the situation declared itself fully.

But some moments do not declare themselves.

They pass.

And what remains is not only the outcome, but the awareness that something could have been done and was not.

This awareness did not collapse into immediate regret. It settled into something more enduring—a recognition of omission. Not what he had done, but what he had not done.

And the realization that in some moments, what is not done carries as much weight as what is.

The moment did not end when it passed. It continued—not as replay, but as question.

What would have happened if I had acted?

The question did not have an answer.

But it remained.

And in remaining, it began to shape how he understood hesitation—not as absence, but as participation.

Not neutral.

But consequential.

PART 2—OMISSION, REGRET, AND THE STRUCTURE OF "I SHOULD HAVE. . ."

The experience described in the previous section centers on a form of moral engagement defined not by action, but by its absence. The individual is present within the moment. They recognize that something is occurring that may require response. And yet, no action is taken. The sequence continues, the moment passes, and the outcome unfolds without interruption. What remains is not the memory of something done, but the awareness that something was not done.

This introduces a distinct pathway within moral injury.

In situations of perpetration, the individual is connected to what they have done. In situations of witnessing, the individual is connected to what they have seen. In omission, the individual is connected to what they did not do. The moral tension does not arise from action or exposure, but from the recognition of unrealized possibility.

Omission is not the absence of awareness.

It occurs in the presence of recognition.

The individual perceives that something could be done, or should be done, even if that perception is incomplete or not fully articulated. The moment contains a point of potential response. The individual is aware of it, even if only partially. And yet, that potential is not acted upon.

This creates a particular form of tension.

At the level of meaning, the individual recognizes that the moment carried significance. This recognition may not have been fully formed at the time, but it becomes clearer in retrospect. The individual returns to the moment and identifies the point at which something different might have occurred. What was initially experienced as ambiguity takes shape as missed possibility.

Meaning, in omission, is often retrospective.

It develops after the moment has passed, as the individual revisits the sequence and identifies what was present but not acted upon.

At the level of obligation, the tension becomes more defined. The individual experiences a sense that action should have been taken. This sense may not have been fully accessible in the moment. It may emerge only afterward, as the individual reconstructs the situation with greater clarity.

This is where the language of "should have" forms.

"I should have said something."

"I should have stepped in."

"I should have acted."

These statements are not simply expressions of regret.

They are attempts to locate obligation after the fact.

At the level of judgment, the individual evaluates the moment in light of what is now understood. The conditions of the situation are reconsidered. The reasons for hesitation are examined. The individual may acknowledge that uncertainty was present, that the situation was complex, that the outcome was not clear.

And yet, the evaluation does not resolve into neutrality.

The individual may understand why they did not act.

But still feel that they should have.

This creates tension between explanation and evaluation.

Understanding the reasons for inaction does not eliminate the sense that action was required.

At the level of agency, the focus shifts to what might have been possible. The individual re-enters the moment, not as it was experienced, but as it is now understood. They identify the point at which intervention could have occurred. They consider what action might have looked like, what effect it might have had, how the sequence might have changed.

This is the structure of counterfactual thinking.

The individual constructs an alternative version of the event—one in which they acted differently and the outcome is altered as a result. This reconstruction is not necessarily accurate. It is shaped by hindsight, by information that was not fully available in the moment, by an understanding of the outcome that did not exist at the time.

And yet, it carries weight.

Because it reveals that action was possible, even if it was not taken.

At the level of legacy, the experience of omission becomes persistent. The individual does not simply remember the moment. They return to it. The "I should have. . ." statement becomes a point of reference, shaping how the moment is understood each time it is revisited.

This repetition is not accidental.

It reflects the fact that the experience has not resolved.

Unlike action, which can be evaluated and integrated, omission leaves an open structure. There is no action to examine directly, only the absence of action and the possibility that was not realized. This absence does not provide closure. It invites return.

Over time, the individual may recognize patterns. The moment of hesitation in one situation may not be isolated. It may be part of a broader way of engaging uncertainty—waiting for clarity, delaying action until the situation becomes more defined, prioritizing stability over interruption.

This recognition deepens the experience.

The individual is no longer only considering a single missed moment.

They are considering a pattern of hesitation.

This is where omission becomes more than situational.

It becomes structural.

The individual begins to ask not only what happened in that moment, but how they tend to respond in moments like it. They may recognize that hesitation is not random, but shaped by prior experience, by role expectations, by an orientation toward caution in the face of uncertainty.

This does not resolve the tension.

It clarifies it.

The experience of omission, then, is not defined solely by regret.

Regret is part of it, but it is not the whole.

What is present is a more complex structure—recognition, hesitation, inaction, and retrospective evaluation. The "I should have. . ." statement is where these elements converge. It is both a conclusion and an opening, both a judgment about the past and a question about what was possible.

It does not close the moment.

It keeps it active.

This is what distinguishes omission from other pathways of moral injury.

In perpetration, the individual seeks to understand what they did and why. In witnessing, they seek to understand what they saw and how to carry it. In omission, the individual returns to what did not occur, to a moment that contained potential that was not realized.

The tension is not located in action.

It is located in absence.

And absence, once recognized, does not easily resolve.

It remains as possibility.

Unrealized.

Revisited.

Carried forward in the form of a question that does not fully close.

What would have happened if I had acted?

PART 3—THE STRUCTURE OF "I SHOULD HAVE. . ."

The moment did not present itself as a decision.

It presented as uncertainty.

He was present within the situation, aware that something was unfolding that required attention, but without a clear directive about what should be done. The elements of the moment did not align into a single, obvious course of action. There were competing demands, incomplete information, and no clarity about what intervention would accomplish or cost.

He recognized that something was happening, but not what it required of him.

At the level of meaning, the moment registered as significant, but not decisive. There was a sense that something might be wrong, or might become wrong, but the conditions were not yet clear enough to define the situation fully. The recognition was partial—enough to create awareness, but not enough to compel immediate action. This partial recognition shaped the experience. It did not demand movement. It allowed hesitation.

At the level of obligation, the question formed but did not fully take shape. There was no clear sense that action was required—only that something could be done, or might be done. This distinction mattered. The absence of necessity created space, and within that space, delay became possible. He did not decide not to act. He allowed the moment to continue.

At the level of judgment, the situation remained open. He evaluated what was happening in real time, but the evaluation did not resolve into a clear conclusion. There were reasons to wait, to observe, to gather more information before acting. These reasons were not incorrect, but they were incomplete. The evaluation produced a provisional understanding that more clarity might emerge if the moment was allowed to develop.

This is where hesitation stabilizes—not as avoidance, but as deferral.

At the level of agency, the individual remained capable of acting, but that capacity was not activated. The possibility of intervention was present but not engaged. Action required a threshold of clarity the situation did not provide. Without that clarity, he did not move.

He waited.

Not indefinitely. Just long enough—long enough for the moment to move beyond the point at which intervention would have been effective. The sequence continued. The opportunity closed.

At the level of outcome, the situation resolved into what it would become. What had been potential became fixed. The moment no longer contained multiple possible directions. It contained a single outcome, shaped by the absence of intervention as much as by the actions that occurred. From the outside, nothing marked the shift. The moment passed.

But the structure of the experience changed.

At the level of retrospective meaning, he returned to the moment with new information. The outcome provided clarity that had not been available at the time. What had been ambiguous became defined. What had been uncertain became interpretable. The moment could now be seen differently. He identified the point at which something could have been done—the opening visible in retrospect, small, brief, but real.

At the level of retrospective obligation, the sense of what should have been done emerged with greater force. What had been tentative in the moment became defined after the fact. The situation was no longer experienced as uncertain, but as one in which action had been possible and should have been taken.

This is where the language forms.

"I should have said something."

The statement did not arrive as a conclusion.

It arrived as recognition.

At the level of retrospective judgment, he evaluated the moment again with the benefit of hindsight. The reasons for hesitation were reconsidered. The uncertainty was re-examined. The lack of clarity was weighed against the outcome that had occurred. The reasons still held, but they no longer resolved the tension. Understanding why he had not acted did not eliminate the sense that he should have. The moment could be explained, but not settled.

At the level of retrospective agency, he engaged in counterfactual thinking, reconstructing the moment as it might have unfolded if he had acted differently. He imagined what could have been said, how the sequence might have shifted, what effect that intervention might have had. These reconstructions could not be verified, but they carried weight because they revealed that action had been possible, even if it had not been taken.

At the level of legacy, the experience did not resolve into a single instance of regret. It became a reference point. The "I should have. . ." statement did not remain attached only to that moment. It extended into others—different situations, different contexts, but the same structure: recognition, hesitation, inaction, retrospective clarity.

"I should have. . ."

The repetition revealed a pattern. The moment was not isolated. It was representative.

The individual saw that hesitation was not only situational, but structural. It reflected a way of engaging uncertainty—waiting for clarity before acting, allowing moments to develop before intervening, prioritizing stability over disruption. This orientation had value. It prevented impulsive action. It respected complexity. But in certain moments, it delayed action beyond the point at which it could make a difference.

This is where omission takes shape as moral experience—not in the absence of care, but in the timing of response.

The individual did not fail to recognize the moment. He recognized it. He did not refuse to act. He delayed. And in that delay, the moment moved beyond him.

The "I should have. . ." statement is not only about what was missed.

It is about when it was missed—the threshold between possibility and closure. Once crossed, it cannot be reopened.

He returns to that threshold not to change it, but to understand it. Where was the opening? What prevented movement? What would it take to respond differently?

These questions do not resolve the past.

They shape the future.

But in the present, the experience remains—not as a single moment, but as a structure: recognition without action, possibility without movement, clarity after the fact.

And a sentence that does not close.

"I should have. . ."

PART 4—REFRAMING MISSED ACTION

When a moment passes without action, the instinct is often to return to it in search of correction. The individual revisits the sequence, identifies the point at which intervention might have occurred, and attempts to determine what should have been done differently. This return is not inherently problematic. It reflects an effort to understand the experience. But when it becomes fixed around a single conclusion—"I should have. . ."—it limits the ability to engage the moment constructively.

The task is not to eliminate the recognition that something was missed.

It is to work with it.

The first movement is recognition. Recognition involves acknowledging that a moment contained a point of potential action that was not taken. This is not a general sense of regret, but a specific identification: there was an opening, and I did not move within it. Naming this clearly prevents the experience from becoming diffuse. It locates the tension in a particular moment rather than allowing it to spread across unrelated experiences.

Recognition also prevents avoidance. Without it, the individual may minimize the significance of the moment or dismiss it as unavoidable. While this can reduce immediate discomfort, it leaves the structure of the experience unexamined.

The second movement is differentiation. In omission, there is a tendency to collapse the entire outcome of the situation into personal responsibility. The individual may interpret the final result as something they caused through inaction. Differentiation interrupts this collapse. It distinguishes between what was within the individual's control and what was not.

This involves holding two statements together: there was something I could have done, and there were elements I could not control. These are not mutually exclusive. The moment contained both.

Differentiation allows the individual to engage their role without expanding it beyond its actual boundaries.

The third movement is accurate location of responsibility. Once differentiation has taken place, the question becomes more precise: what, in this moment, was mine to do? This question is not answered abstractly. It requires returning to the conditions of the moment as they were experienced, not as they are understood after the fact.

What information was available?

What constraints were present?

What would action have required at that point?

This process does not eliminate the possibility that action was warranted. It clarifies the conditions under which that action would have occurred.

Accurate location prevents two distortions: assuming total responsibility for the outcome, or denying responsibility entirely. Both remove the individual from the actual structure of the moment.

The fourth movement is engaging counterfactual thinking with discipline. The "I should have. . ." statement is often accompanied by imagined alternatives—scenarios in which the individual acted differently and the outcome improved as a result. These reconstructions can reveal that action was possible, but they are shaped by hindsight. They incorporate knowledge that was not fully available in the moment.

Engaging this process constructively requires holding its limits. The question is not what would have happened if I had acted, but what was realistically possible given what I knew and the conditions I was in. This reframes counterfactual thinking from speculative correction to informed reflection.

The fifth movement is acknowledging limitation without collapsing into resignation. In many instances of omission, the individual delayed action because the situation did not provide sufficient clarity. This lack of clarity is part of the structure of the moment, not simply a failure of perception.

Acknowledging limitation involves recognizing that the moment did not present itself as decisively as it may appear in retrospect. The individual acted within uncertainty. This does not remove the possibility that action was warranted, but it situates the hesitation within the conditions that produced it.

The sixth movement is shifting from evaluation of the past to orientation toward the future. The "I should have. . ." statement is oriented backward. It evaluates what did not occur. While this evaluation is necessary, it cannot change the moment.

Reframing involves asking a different question: what does this moment reveal about how I respond to uncertainty? This shifts the focus from the specific instance to the pattern it represents. The individual is no longer only evaluating what was missed, but examining how similar moments may be approached differently in the future.

This is not a commitment to act in every uncertain situation.

It is a commitment to recognize when hesitation is shaping the response.

The seventh movement is integrating the experience without allowing it to define identity. Omission can easily become personalized in a way that extends beyond the moment. The individual may move from "I should have acted" to "I am someone who fails to act." This shift transforms a specific experience into a general conclusion about the self.

Integration interrupts this expansion. It holds the experience within its context. The moment is significant, but it is not definitive. It is part of a broader pattern of action and inaction, not a total description of the individual.

Integration allows the experience to remain instructive without becoming determinative.

Reframing missed action, then, is not about resolving the past.

It is about engaging it accurately.

From undifferentiated regret to specific recognition.

From collapsed responsibility to clear boundaries.

From speculative alternatives to grounded reflection.

From fixation on what was missed to awareness of how moments are navigated.

The "I should have. . ." statement does not disappear.

But it changes.

It becomes less of a conclusion and more of an entry point—a way of identifying where a moment contained potential that was not realized.

The moment cannot be reopened.

But it can be understood.

And in that understanding, the next moment is encountered differently.

REFLECTION

When you return to a moment where you did not act, what stands out most clearly?

Is it the outcome, or the point at which action might have been possible?

How do you describe that moment to yourself?

Does your language remain specific—tied to that moment—or does it expand into broader conclusions about who you are?

What did you recognize in the moment, even if only partially?

What prevented that recognition from becoming action?

Was it uncertainty, timing, role, consequence—or something harder to name?

When you say, "I should have. . .," what are you actually locating?

A missed opportunity?

A clearer understanding that came too late?

A standard you now see more fully than you could in the moment?

How do you hold the reasons you did not act?

Do they still make sense?

Do they explain the moment without resolving it?

What assumptions shape how you imagine the moment might have unfolded differently?

What do you assume would have changed?

What do you assume would have remained the same?

Where do you see this pattern elsewhere?

Not only this moment—but others.

Recognition.

Pause.

Delay.

And afterward, the same sentence.

"I should have. . ."

What conditions tend to produce hesitation for you?

What do you wait for before acting?

Clarity?

Certainty?

Permission?

What would it mean to recognize those conditions earlier, without requiring the moment to fully declare itself?

How do you carry omission?

As a fixed conclusion?

Or as a point of understanding that shapes how you meet the next moment?

WHAT'S AHEAD

We have seen how what was not done can remain as powerfully as what was.

Next, we will explore disorientation—when the framework itself begins to shift or collapse.

Chapter 9

Disorientation

PART 1—WHEN THINGS STOP MAKING SENSE

It did not begin with a crisis.

It began with a shift.

Nothing in the moment announced itself as different. The situation unfolded as others had before—familiar structures, recognizable patterns, roles that had been inhabited many times. There was no immediate disruption, no visible break in the sequence. From the outside, everything appeared intact.

And yet, something was not aligning.

He noticed it slowly—not as a clear realization, but as a subtle friction between what he expected to understand and what he was actually experiencing. The categories he relied on to interpret the moment were present, but they did not hold as they had before. They seemed to apply, and yet not fully. Something fit, but not completely.

At first, this did not register as a problem.

It felt like complexity.

Situations are often complex. They do not always resolve cleanly. There are tensions, competing interpretations, incomplete information. He had encountered this before. He knew how to hold uncertainty, how to wait for additional clarity, how to allow a situation to develop before drawing conclusions.

So he stayed with it, continuing to observe, interpret, and engage the moment using the frameworks that had guided him in the past.

But the friction remained.

It did not resolve into clarity.

It did not deepen into understanding.

It persisted.

He began to notice that the difficulty was not only in the situation itself, but in his ability to make sense of it. The usual pathways of interpretation—those that had previously allowed him to organize what he was seeing into something coherent—no longer produced the same result. He could describe what was happening, identify the elements, and follow the sequence.

But he could not bring it together.

The situation did not lack detail.

It lacked coherence.

This is where the shift became more visible. He was no longer only encountering a complex situation; he was encountering a breakdown in understanding. The moment no longer held together in the way it had before.

He tried to stabilize it.

That is what we do. When something does not make sense, we reach for what has made sense before—familiar categories, trusted frameworks, known interpretations. We attempt to bring the moment back into alignment with what we already understand.

He did the same. He named what he could name, organized what he could organize, interpreted what he could interpret.

But each attempt only held part of the experience.

Never the whole.

There was always something left over—something that did not fit.

At first, this appeared as a minor disruption: a detail that resisted explanation, a tension that could not be fully resolved. But over time, it expanded. The gap between what he was experiencing and what he could make sense of began to widen.

The frameworks did not collapse all at once.

They thinned.

They held in some places.

They failed in others.

He could still use them.

But he could no longer rely on them.

This is where disorientation begins—not in the absence of meaning, but in the instability of it.

He was still interpreting the situation, but his interpretations no longer settled. They shifted. What seemed clear in one moment became uncertain in the next. What felt stable began to move. He noticed it in small ways—conclusions that did not hold, explanations that did not resolve, a sense that what he was seeing could not be fully contained within the categories he had available.

He began to question his own interpretation—not dramatically, but persistently.

Am I understanding this correctly?

The question did not produce an answer.

It produced more questioning.

He returned to the situation, attempting to clarify it, to stabilize it, to bring it into alignment with something that would hold. But each return produced the same result—partial clarity, incomplete resolution, a sense that something essential remained just outside of what he could grasp.

This did not immediately create distress.

It created unease.

A subtle sense that something was shifting beneath the surface of the experience.

He continued to engage, interpret, and move within the situation. But now there was an added layer—not only what was happening, but his inability to fully make sense of it.

This is where the experience began to change.

He was no longer only responding to the situation.

He was responding to the loss of coherence within it.

The moment no longer held together.

And neither did his understanding of it.

He noticed the effect this had on him—not in the moment itself, but afterward, in reflection, when he attempted to explain what had happened. He could describe the sequence and identify the events, but when he tried to articulate what it meant, the explanation did not hold. It shifted, fractured, and refused to settle into a single, stable account. He would say one thing and then revise it—not because he had been wrong, but because no single explanation fully contained the experience.

He began to feel the instability—not as confusion in the sense of not knowing anything, but as the inability to hold what he knew together.

This is different.

He was not without understanding.

He was without coherence.

The distinction matters. He knew what had happened. He did not know how to make sense of it.

This is where disorientation moves from situation to experience. It is no longer about what is happening, but about the breakdown in the ability to interpret it.

He returned again to the moment, trying to name it, to settle it, to bring it into alignment with something that would hold. But each attempt produced the same result—something fit, something did not. The moment would not resolve.

And in not resolving, it began to alter how he trusted his own understanding.

If the frameworks do not hold here, where else do they not hold?

The question extended beyond the moment. It reached into other experiences, other interpretations, other assumptions that had previously felt stable.

This is how disorientation spreads—not by overwhelming the individual all at once, but by introducing instability into the structures that organize experience.

He did not lose all meaning.

He lost confidence in it.

The shift was subtle.

But it was significant.

He continued to function.

He continued to respond.

But now there was a gap between what he was doing and how he understood what he was doing.

The gap did not close.

It remained.

And in remaining, it began to shape the experience itself.

He was no longer only in the moment.

He was also outside of it—watching his own attempts to understand it, noticing where they held and where they did not.

The moment did not collapse.

But it no longer held.

And that difference changed everything.

PART 2—WHEN MEANING FRAMEWORKS NO LONGER HOLD

The experience described in the previous section centers on a disruption not of action, but of understanding. The individual remains present within the situation. They continue to observe, interpret, and engage. And yet, the frameworks that once allowed them to organize experience into something coherent no longer function in the same way. What remains intact at the level of detail begins to fragment at the level of meaning.

This introduces a distinct pathway within moral injury.

In situations of perpetration, the tension emerges from what one has done. In witnessing, it emerges from what one has seen. In omission, it emerges from what one did not do. In disorientation, the tension emerges from the inability to make sense of what is being encountered.

The problem is not only the situation.

It is the loss of a stable way to interpret it.

Meaning frameworks are the structures through which individuals organize experience. They include moral categories, role expectations, theological commitments, professional training, and prior experience. These frameworks do not eliminate complexity, but they provide a way of holding it. They allow the individual to say: this is what is happening, this is what it means, this is how I respond.

In disorientation, these functions begin to break down—not all at once, and not completely. The frameworks remain available, but they no longer produce coherence. They apply in part, but not in full. They explain some elements of the situation, but leave others unaccounted for. The individual continues to use them, but with diminishing confidence in their ability to hold the whole.

At the level of meaning, this breakdown appears as fragmentation. The individual can still identify what is occurring, describe events, name actions, and recognize outcomes. But these elements no longer organize into a stable interpretation. The connections between them weaken. The narrative that would normally hold them together does not fully form.

Meaning is not absent.

It is unstable.

At the level of obligation, the disruption becomes more complex. In previous pathways, the individual can ask what should be done or what should have been done. In disorientation, that question becomes difficult to answer because the conditions that would guide the answer are no longer clear.

If the situation cannot be fully understood, then the basis for obligation becomes uncertain. The individual may still feel that something is required, but they cannot clearly determine what that is.

This produces a different kind of tension—not between action and inaction, but between expectation and uncertainty.

At the level of judgment, the individual attempts to evaluate what is happening, but the evaluation does not settle. The categories used to determine what is right or wrong, appropriate or inappropriate, sufficient or insufficient, do not align cleanly with the situation. The individual may reach a conclusion, only to find that it does not hold when the situation is considered from another angle.

Judgment becomes provisional.

It shifts.

Not because the individual lacks conviction.

But because the situation resists stable interpretation.

At the level of agency, the individual remains capable of acting, but the basis for action becomes unclear. In the absence of a stable interpretation, it becomes difficult to determine what action would be appropriate or effective. The individual may continue to act, but with less confidence in the meaning of those actions.

Action continues.

Clarity does not.

This creates a gap between behavior and understanding. The individual remains engaged in the situation, but no longer fully grounded in a clear sense of what that engagement means.

At the level of legacy, the effects of disorientation extend beyond the immediate moment. The instability introduced into the meaning framework does not remain confined to a single situation. It begins to influence how other experiences are interpreted.

If meaning does not hold here, where else does it not hold?

This question is not always articulated directly, but it shapes the experience. The individual may revisit prior assumptions, reconsider interpretations that once felt stable, and question the reliability of the frameworks they have depended on.

This does not lead to immediate collapse.

It introduces doubt.

Not about everything.

But about enough to disrupt coherence.

Disorientation, then, is not defined by the absence of meaning.

It is defined by the instability of it.

The individual continues to interpret, but those interpretations no longer settle into a form that can be relied upon. They remain in motion, shifting as the situation is reconsidered from different angles.

This is why disorientation is often difficult to identify. From the outside, the individual may appear to be functioning normally. They continue to engage, respond, and make decisions. The disruption is not in behavior, but in the underlying structure of understanding.

Internally, however, the experience is different. There is a growing awareness that the frameworks that once provided stability no longer hold in the same way. The individual may not abandon them, but they no longer trust them fully.

This partial loss of trust is significant. It alters how experience is held. It changes how meaning is constructed. It introduces a layer of uncertainty into situations that would previously have been interpreted with confidence.

The individual is not without resources.

They are without coherence.

This distinction is central. Disorientation does not remove the capacity to think, interpret, or act. It disrupts the ability to bring those capacities together into a stable understanding.

The experience is not one of emptiness.

It is one of fragmentation.

Elements remain.

Connections weaken.

The individual continues to engage the situation, but without the same confidence that their understanding will hold.

This creates a persistent tension—not between competing actions, but between competing interpretations. The individual may hold multiple possible explanations at once, none of which fully resolves the experience. Each offers partial clarity. None provides complete coherence.

This is where disorientation becomes morally significant. It affects not only how the individual understands the situation, but how they understand themselves within it. If meaning cannot be stabilized, then identity—often constructed through stable interpretations of experience—becomes more difficult to maintain.

The question shifts.

Not only what is happening?

But what does it mean?

And if that cannot be answered with stability—

What does that mean for how I understand my role, my responsibility, my place within this situation?

These questions do not resolve easily.

They remain open.

And in remaining open, they shape the experience of disorientation itself.

PART 3—WHEN UNDERSTANDING FRACTURES

The moment did not present as incomprehensible.

It presented as incomplete.

He was able to describe what was happening. The elements of the situation were visible. The sequence could be followed. There were actions, responses, and decisions that could be identified and named. Nothing was hidden. Nothing was inaccessible.

And yet, the experience did not come together.

At the level of meaning, the situation registered as significant but unsettled. He recognized that something important was occurring, but he could not determine what that significance was. The details were present, but they did not organize into a clear interpretation. Each element made sense on its own. Together, they did not resolve.

This created a form of tension that was not immediately identifiable—not confusion, not lack of information, but lack of coherence.

At the level of obligation, the difficulty deepened. He could not determine what the situation required of him because he could not determine what the situation was. The usual connection between understanding and response weakened. He remained aware that something mattered, but he could not locate what action, if any, would be appropriate.

The question did not resolve.

What should I do?

It remained open.

At the level of judgment, he attempted to evaluate what was happening. He considered the actions of others, the conditions of the situation, and the possible interpretations that might bring clarity. Each attempt produced a partial result. One interpretation explained one aspect. Another explained a different aspect.

None held the whole.

He could move between them.

But he could not settle in any one of them.

This is where fragmentation becomes visible—not in the absence of interpretation, but in the inability of interpretation to hold.

At the level of agency, he continued to act. The situation did not pause. Decisions still needed to be made. Responses still needed to be given. He acted as he could, drawing on the frameworks that had guided him in the past.

But the relationship between action and understanding had shifted.

He was no longer acting from a stable interpretation.

He was acting within instability.

The actions themselves were not necessarily different.

The experience of acting was.

There was less confidence that what he was doing aligned with what was actually required, less certainty that his responses were grounded in a clear understanding of the situation.

Action continued.

But it no longer resolved the experience.

At the level of outcome, the situation moved forward. Events unfolded into what they would become. From the outside, the sequence appeared intact. The moment passed as others had passed.

But the experience did not settle.

It did not integrate.

At the level of retrospective meaning, he returned to the moment and attempted to bring it into coherence. He reviewed the sequence, reconsidered the interpretations, and tried to construct a narrative that would hold the elements together.

The effort did not fail.

It remained incomplete.

Each attempt clarified something.

But never everything.

The moment could be understood in parts.

It could not be held as a whole.

At the level of retrospective obligation, the question of what should have been done remained unresolved. Unlike omission, where the individual can identify a missed action, disorientation does not provide a clear alternative. There is no single point at which action can be located and evaluated.

The uncertainty that was present in the moment remains present afterward.

The question persists.

But it does not sharpen.

At the level of retrospective judgment, he continued to evaluate the situation, but the evaluation did not stabilize. What seemed sufficient from one perspective appeared inadequate from another. What seemed justified under one interpretation seemed questionable under another.

The conclusions shifted—not because he lacked conviction, but because no single interpretation could account for the experience.

At the level of retrospective agency, there was no clear counterfactual. He could imagine different actions, but without a stable interpretation of the situation, he could not determine whether those actions would have been more appropriate.

The usual structure of "I should have. . ." did not form.

Instead, a different pattern emerged.

"I don't know what should have happened."

This statement did not resolve the experience.

It named its structure.

At the level of legacy, the effects of disorientation extended beyond the moment. The instability in understanding did not remain confined to that situation. It began to influence how he approached other experiences.

He noticed a shift—a hesitation not only in action, but in interpretation. A tendency to hold multiple possibilities without settling into one. A reduced confidence that his understanding would hold across different contexts.

This did not prevent engagement.

But it altered it.

He remained present.

But less certain.

He continued to interpret.

But less convinced.

The frameworks were still there.

But they no longer carried the same authority.

This is how disorientation becomes structural—not through a single overwhelming event, but through repeated encounters with situations that resist coherence. Each instance reinforces the sense that understanding may not hold, that interpretation may not resolve, that meaning may remain unstable.

Over time, this changes how the individual relates to experience itself—not only what is happening, but how it can be understood.

The individual is no longer only engaging the situation.

He is engaging the limits of his own interpretation.

The moment does not collapse.

But it does not hold.

And in that gap, something shifts.

Not the loss of all meaning.

But the loss of confidence that meaning can be stabilized.

PART 4—REBUILDING COHERENCE

When meaning begins to fragment, the instinct is often to restore it as quickly as possible. The individual seeks resolution, attempts to stabilize interpretation, and looks for an explanation that will bring the experience back into alignment with what has previously held. This impulse is understandable. Coherence enables action, judgment, and a sense of orientation within the situation.

But when coherence is forced too quickly, it comes at the cost of accuracy.

The task is not to eliminate uncertainty.

It is to work within it.

The first movement is recognition. Recognition involves acknowledging that the experience is not lacking information, but lacking coherence. The individual can describe what has occurred, but cannot bring those elements together into a stable interpretation. Naming this distinction prevents the experience from being misidentified as confusion or failure.

It is not that nothing is understood.

It is that what is understood does not yet hold together.

Recognition allows the individual to remain engaged without forcing premature conclusions.

The second movement is differentiation. In disorientation, there is a tendency to collapse the instability of meaning into a failure of self. The individual may question their ability to interpret, to judge, to understand. Differentiation interrupts this collapse by distinguishing between the limits of the situation and the limits of the individual.

Some situations resist coherence.

This does not mean the individual is incapable of understanding.

It means the situation cannot yet be organized into a stable form.

Differentiation allows the individual to maintain trust in their capacity to interpret, even when interpretation does not settle.

The third movement is holding multiple interpretations without forcing resolution. When coherence is unstable, the individual may encounter several possible explanations for what is occurring. Each may account for part of the situation. None may account for all of it.

The impulse is to select one and commit to it.

Rebuilding coherence requires resisting that impulse.

Instead, the individual holds these interpretations in tension, allowing each to remain present without requiring that one resolve the others. This is not indecision. It is disciplined openness to the complexity of the situation.

Coherence, in this stage, is not singular.

It is provisional.

The fourth movement is locating stable elements within the instability. Even when overall meaning does not hold, certain aspects of the situation remain clear. Actions can be identified. Effects can be observed. Values can still be recognized, even if they do not fully organize the situation.

Rebuilding coherence involves anchoring in what remains stable.

What do I know?

What remains clear, even as other elements shift?

These anchors do not resolve the whole, but they provide points of orientation within it.

The fifth movement is allowing coherence to emerge rather than forcing it. In many cases, meaning stabilizes over time as additional information becomes available, as the individual revisits the situation, and as connections that were not initially visible begin to form.

This process cannot be accelerated without distortion.

Allowing coherence to emerge requires patience—a willingness to remain within partial understanding without resolving it prematurely.

This is not passive.

It is active restraint.

The sixth movement is re-engaging interpretation in community. Disorientation intensifies when the individual attempts to resolve it in isolation. Without external perspectives, the instability of interpretation deepens, and the individual may cycle through the same partial explanations without reaching greater clarity.

Bringing the experience into relationship allows multiple interpretive frameworks to be engaged. Others may see connections the individual does not, or help stabilize elements that feel uncertain.

The goal is not to arrive at a single agreed-upon interpretation.

It is to expand the capacity to hold the experience.

The seventh movement is integrating instability without allowing it to collapse meaning entirely. Disorientation can lead to a broader conclusion that meaning itself is unreliable. The individual may begin to question not only the current situation, but the validity of interpretation more generally.

Integration resists this expansion. It acknowledges that some situations resist coherence without concluding that all meaning is unstable. The experience is held within its context. It becomes part of how the individual understands the limits of interpretation, not evidence that interpretation itself is no longer possible.

Rebuilding coherence, then, is not about restoring certainty.

It is about restoring the capacity to engage meaning without requiring it to fully resolve.

From fragmentation to provisional structure.

From forced conclusions to disciplined openness.

From isolation to shared interpretation.

From instability to anchored engagement.

The experience does not become simple.

It becomes livable.

The individual is no longer waiting for the moment to make complete sense. They are learning to remain within it, to act within it, and to interpret within it—even when that interpretation remains incomplete.

Coherence returns.

Not as certainty.

But as the ability to hold what does not fully resolve.

REFLECTION

When you encounter a situation that does not make sense, what is your first response?

Do you move quickly to resolve it?

Or do you remain with it?

How do you distinguish between not understanding something and not being able to bring your understanding into coherence?

What elements of the situation remain clear, even when the whole does not hold?

Where do you find yourself forcing conclusions in order to reduce uncertainty?

What happens when you allow multiple interpretations to remain present?

Do you experience that as clarity—or as instability?

What assumptions shape your need for resolution?

What do you believe must happen in order for something to "make sense"?

When your usual frameworks do not hold, how do you respond?

Do you abandon them?

Reinforce them?

Or begin to question them?

What happens to your sense of responsibility when you cannot clearly determine what is required?

How do you act when understanding does not settle?

What changes when you bring the experience into conversation with others?

What do they see that you do not?

What do they hold differently?

How do you carry situations that do not resolve?

As problems to be solved?

Or as experiences to be held?

What would it mean to trust your capacity to interpret, even when interpretation remains incomplete?

WHAT'S AHEAD

We have seen how moral injury can unsettle meaning itself.

Next, we will move into context—how these experiences take shape within real-world environments.

SECTION III

Contexts of Moral Injury

Chapter 10

Disaster Response

PART 1—TRIAGE AND IMPOSSIBLE CHOICES

IT DID NOT BEGIN with a single decision.

It began with too many.

The scene did not present itself as one problem to be solved, but as a field of competing needs, each demanding attention at the same time. There was no sequence that allowed for careful consideration, no clear order in which things could be addressed. Everything was immediate. Everything mattered. And not everything could be done.

He moved into the space already aware of this. Training had prepared him for it. The language was familiar—triage, prioritization, limited resources. These were not new concepts. They were part of the structure of response, a way to act when the situation exceeded capacity.

But knowing the structure is not the same as inhabiting it.

In the moment, abstraction fell away. What remained were people—voices, faces, conditions that did not wait.

He began to assess. That is what the training required: quick evaluation, immediate categorization. Who needs intervention now? Who can wait? Who cannot be helped?

The questions were clear.

The answers were not.

He moved from one person to the next, gathering what information he could, making determinations based on what was visible and what could be known in seconds. There was no time for certainty. Decisions were made within incomplete understanding. He acted, directed, and moved on.

Each decision closed something—not only a course of action, but a set of possibilities that would not be pursued.

This is the structure of triage: to act here is to not act there; to give attention in one direction is to withhold it from another. The logic is necessary. The cost is real.

He did not stop to consider the cost.

He could not.

The situation did not allow for reflection. It required movement.

He continued—one assessment to the next, one decision to the next—each made under pressure, each made with limits. There were not enough resources, not enough time, not enough capacity to meet every need.

This was not a failure of response.

It was the condition of it.

He knew this.

And still, the weight accumulated—not in a single moment, but across them. A decision here, another there, each justified within the framework, each necessary, and each leaving something unaddressed.

He began to notice the pattern—not consciously, not in a way that could be articulated in the moment, but as a shift in how the experience was held. He was not only responding.

He was choosing between outcomes.

Not ideal outcomes.

Possible ones.

The question was no longer what is the right thing to do?

It became:

What can be done, given what is available?

The difference is subtle.

But it changes everything.

He encountered a case that brought the tension into sharper focus. One person required immediate, resource-intensive intervention. Another required less time and fewer resources, but without it, their condition would deteriorate.

He could not do both.

Not fully.

Not at the same time.

The decision did not arrive as a clear directive. There was no internal voice that resolved the tension. There was only the situation—and the need to act within it.

He chose. He directed resources. He moved forward.

The moment did not pause to confirm the decision.

It continued.

And he continued with it.

From the outside, the action was appropriate. It aligned with training. It followed established protocols. It made sense within the structure of response.

But the experience did not end with the decision.

It moved with him—into the next moment, and the next. Each new decision layered onto the previous ones, each shaped by the same conditions: scarcity, time, constraint.

The accumulation did not present as immediate distress.

It presented as compression—a narrowing of the space in which decisions could be made. Less time. Less room for consideration. Less distance between recognition and action.

The decisions did not become easier.

They became faster.

More automatic.

More dependent on the frameworks that had been trained into him.

This is necessary.

Without it, response would stop.

But something else begins to happen.

The distance between action and reflection widens.

He continued to act, but he no longer had access to the full weight of what each decision carried.

That would come later.

For now, the work required continuation. The field did not clear. The needs did not resolve. He moved through them—responding, deciding, moving again.

At some point, the intensity shifted—not ended, but shifted. There was space—not enough for full reflection, but enough for awareness to begin to return.

He began to notice what had been happening—not in detail, but in structure. He had not been making isolated decisions. He had been operating within a system of constraint that required trade-offs at every point.

He had not simply been helping.

He had been choosing.

Between people.

Between needs.

Between outcomes.

The recognition did not resolve into judgment. It remained suspended. He knew the decisions had been necessary. He knew they had followed the structure of response.

And yet, something in the experience resisted closure.

He could not fully settle into the idea that necessity removed the weight of what had been chosen.

He returned, briefly, to one moment—not the most extreme, not the most visible, but one that had required a clear allocation of attention in one direction and not another.

He could see it: the decision, the movement, the consequence.

He did not yet name it.

He did not yet evaluate it.

But he recognized it.

This is where the experience begins to shift—not in the moment of action, but in the awareness that follows. The realization that response under constraint is not only technical.

It is moral.

And that the structure of disaster response does not remove that dimension.

It concentrates it.

PART 2—SCARCITY AND MORAL COMPRESSION

The experience described in the previous section is structured not only by urgency, but by limitation. The individual is not simply responding to need. They are responding to need under conditions where not all needs can be met. The defining feature of the situation is not only intensity, but insufficiency.

There is not enough—time, personnel, resources, or capacity to fully respond to every demand that presents itself.

This introduces a distinct pathway within moral injury.

In situations of perpetration, the tension emerges from what one has done. In witnessing, it emerges from what one has seen. In omission, it emerges from what one did not do. In disorientation, it emerges from the inability to make sense of what is happening. In disaster response under scarcity, the tension emerges from what must be done when not everything can be done.

The problem is not uncertainty.

It is constraint.

Scarcity is not simply a logistical condition.

It is a moral condition.

At the level of meaning, scarcity alters how the situation is understood. The individual no longer encounters need as something that can be fully addressed. Instead, need appears as something that exceeds response. The field of care expands beyond what can be held. The situation is no longer experienced as a set of problems to be solved, but as a set of demands that must be sorted.

Meaning reorganizes around limitation.

The question is no longer what needs to be done?

It becomes:

What can be done?

At the level of obligation, scarcity reshapes what responsibility looks like. Under normal conditions, obligation can be oriented toward meeting needs as they arise. Under scarcity, obligation cannot be fulfilled in full. The individual must act within limits that prevent complete response.

This does not remove obligation.

It fragments it.

The individual experiences multiple, simultaneous obligations that cannot all be honored. Each claim is real. Each demand is valid. But they cannot all be met.

This produces a distinct tension—not between right and wrong, but between competing goods.

At the level of judgment, the individual must evaluate not only what is needed, but what is possible. Decisions are made not on the basis of ideal outcomes, but constrained ones. The criteria for judgment shift. Effectiveness replaces completeness. Priority replaces totality.

The question becomes:

Which action will produce the most impact within the limits that exist?

This is not a neutral shift.

It alters the moral structure of decision-making.

The individual is no longer choosing between good and bad outcomes.

They are choosing between insufficient ones.

At the level of agency, the individual remains active, but their action is bounded. They are capable of responding, but not of responding fully. Each act of care is also an act of limitation. To act in one place is to not act in another. Agency becomes directional rather than comprehensive.

This narrows the field of action—not because the individual is unwilling, but because the situation does not allow otherwise.

At the level of legacy, the effects of scarcity do not remain within the moment. Decisions made under constraint persist. They are remembered not only for what was done, but for what could not be done.

The individual may return to these moments—not to question the necessity of the decisions, but to encounter the unresolved presence of unmet needs.

Scarcity leaves residue.

Not because the decisions were wrong.

But because they were incomplete.

This is where the concept of moral compression becomes visible.

Moral compression refers to the condition in which multiple moral demands are forced into a limited space of time, attention, and capacity. The individual must respond to several competing obligations simultaneously, without the ability to expand the conditions in which those obligations could be fully met.

Time compresses.

Options compress.

Attention compresses.

And within that compression, decisions must still be made.

At the level of experience, this compression produces intensity. There is little space between recognition and response. Decisions are made quickly, often without the opportunity for full reflection. The individual relies on training, protocols, and practiced patterns of response.

This is necessary.

But it changes how decisions are held.

There is less room to process.

Less room to consider.

Less room to feel.

The decision is made.

And the next one follows.

At the level of meaning, moral compression limits the ability to fully integrate what is happening. The individual recognizes that each decision carries weight, but there is insufficient space to hold that weight in the moment.

Meaning is deferred.

Not denied.

But postponed.

At the level of obligation, compression intensifies competing demands. The individual does not encounter one obligation at a time, but several at once. Each calls for response. Each is valid. But they cannot all be engaged fully.

The individual must select.

And in selecting, must leave others unaddressed.

At the level of judgment, compression reduces the time available for evaluation. Decisions are made under pressure, often with incomplete information. Criteria must be applied quickly—sometimes intuitively, sometimes through protocols that stand in for extended deliberation.

This does not eliminate moral reasoning.

It condenses it.

At the level of agency, compression accelerates action. The individual moves from one decision to the next with minimal transition. There is little space between acts. Continuity of action becomes the priority as the situation demands sustained response.

Agency becomes continuous.

But not expansive.

At the level of legacy, moral compression contributes to the accumulation of unresolved experience. Because there is insufficient space to process each decision as it occurs, the weight of those decisions may emerge later, when intensity subsides and reflection becomes possible.

The individual may revisit the sequence—not as it was experienced in the moment, but as it can now be understood with greater distance.

This is where the full moral dimension becomes visible.

Not because it was absent before.

But because there was no space to hold it.

Scarcity and moral compression, then, do not eliminate moral responsibility.

They concentrate it.

They require the individual to act within limits that prevent full response, to make decisions that cannot resolve all demands, and to carry the residual presence of what could not be done.

The tension is not that the individual failed to respond.

It is that response itself was constrained.

And within that constraint, every action carries both necessity and loss.

PART 3—FIELD DECISION UNDER CONSTRAINT

The moment did not present as a single decision.

It presented as a narrowing field.

He had already been moving through multiple cases, each requiring attention, each shaped by the same limits—time, personnel, resources. The pace had not slowed. The flow of need had not diminished. Each decision led directly into the next.

There was no reset.

Only continuation.

He entered the next space with this already in motion. The situation was immediately clear in one sense and unclear in another. He could identify what was in front of him—assess condition, urgency, and likely trajectory. The elements were visible.

But the decision was not singular.

It was comparative.

Two individuals required intervention. One required immediate, resource-intensive care. Without it, deterioration would be rapid. The intervention would demand sustained attention, multiple resources, and time that could not be divided. The other required care that was less intensive but still time-sensitive. Without intervention, their condition would worsen, though not as immediately. The care required was shorter, less resource-intensive, but still necessary.

He could not do both.

Not fully.

Not at the same time.

At the level of meaning, the situation registered not as a question of what was needed, but as recognition that more was needed than could be given. Both cases were legitimate. Both demands were real. The field did not prioritize for him.

He had to do that.

At the level of obligation, the tension became immediate. He was responsible to both. There was no basis for dismissing one as secondary. Each carried its own claim. Each required response.

But the conditions did not allow both claims to be honored simultaneously.

Obligation did not resolve.

It multiplied.

At the level of judgment, he evaluated—assessing severity, likelihood of survival, resource allocation, and time. He drew on training: triage protocols, prior experience, established criteria for prioritization.

The framework was clear.

The application was not neutral.

Each factor pointed in a direction.

None eliminated the tension.

He could justify prioritizing the more critical case. He could justify stabilizing the other first, given the shorter intervention time.

Both decisions had rationale.

Neither removed the cost.

This is where moral compression intensifies—not a choice between right and wrong, but between insufficient options.

At the level of agency, he acted. He chose a direction, allocated resources, and began the intervention. The decision did not resolve the field.

It reorganized it.

Attention moved in one direction.

And in that movement, it was withdrawn from another.

The action was immediate.

The consequence was simultaneous.

He continued the intervention, maintaining focus on the case he had prioritized. The work required concentration. There was no space to revisit the decision in real time. The situation demanded full engagement.

And yet, the presence of the other case did not disappear.

It remained.

Not as a distraction.

But as an awareness.

At the level of experience, the structure becomes visible. He was not only engaged in what he was doing. He was aware of what he was not doing. The two were not separate.

They were linked.

Each moment of attention carried with it the absence of attention elsewhere.

This is the lived form of constraint.

At the level of outcome, the situation moved forward. The intervention progressed. The condition of the individual he had prioritized began to stabilize. From the outside, the sequence appeared effective.

The decision produced a measurable result.

But the field had not resolved.

The other case continued.

Without him.

Without the same level of intervention.

The trajectory there changed.

He became aware of it—not immediately, but as the distance between the two cases became more visible. The condition had worsened—not unexpectedly, but unavoidably.

At the level of retrospective meaning, the structure of the decision took shape. He could see the sequence clearly—the assessment, the evaluation, the choice, the intervention, the outcome.

Each step made sense.

The logic held.

And yet, the experience did not settle into resolution.

He had done what the situation required.

And still, something remained.

At the level of retrospective obligation, the tension did not disappear. He could not say that he had failed to respond. He had acted. He had followed protocol. He had applied training.

But he could not say that all obligations had been met.

Because they had not been.

They could not have been.

This is the structure of scarcity.

The inability to fulfill all demands does not remove their presence.

It preserves it.

At the level of retrospective judgment, he evaluated the decision again. He reconsidered the factors, the timing, the allocation of resources.

The reasoning remained sound.

The conclusion did not change.

But the experience did.

The decision could be justified.

It could not be neutralized.

At the level of retrospective agency, there was no single counterfactual that resolved the situation. He could imagine choosing differently—reversing the order, redistributing attention—but each alternative carried its own limitation, its own cost, and its own set of unmet needs.

There was no version of the moment in which all outcomes were satisfied.

The structure itself prevented it.

At the level of legacy, the experience did not remain contained within the moment. It became a reference point—not only for what had been done, but for how decisions are made under constraint.

He recognized that this was not an isolated case.

It was representative.

The conditions would repeat.

The structure would recur.

The necessity to choose between legitimate needs would not disappear.

He was not only remembering the moment.

He was recognizing the pattern.

This is where disaster response reveals its deeper dimension. It is not only the presence of need.

It is the inevitability of limitation.

The responder is not only acting.

He is allocating.

Not only helping.

But choosing where help will go—and where it will not.

The decision did not fail.

The situation did not resolve.

And in that space between necessity and insufficiency, something remained—not confusion, not uncertainty, but the recognition that every action carried both care and loss.

PART 4—WORKING UNDER CONSTRAINT: MIR + M.O.R.A.L IN DISASTER CARE

When decisions must be made under conditions of scarcity, the instinct is to move past them as quickly as possible. The work demands continuation.

The field does not allow pause. The next need presents itself immediately, and attention must shift.

But what is not processed in the moment does not disappear.

It accumulates.

The task is not to eliminate the constraints of the field.

It is to work within them in a way that preserves clarity, integrity, and the capacity to continue.

The first movement is recognition. Recognition involves naming the condition of the situation accurately. The responder is not failing to meet need. The responder is operating within a field where need exceeds capacity.

This distinction is essential.

It is not that I did not do enough.

It is that not everything could be done.

Recognition interrupts the tendency to interpret limitation as failure. It locates the experience within the structure of disaster response and allows the responder to remain engaged without misidentifying the nature of the work.

The second movement is differentiating between necessity and preference. Under normal conditions, decisions may be guided by what would be ideal. In disaster response, decisions are guided by what is possible. The responder must distinguish between what would have been preferred and what the situation allowed.

This does not diminish the value of what could not be done.

It clarifies the conditions under which decisions were made.

The third movement is applying MIR in real time. MIR—Minimize, Interpret, Re-engage—provides a way of stabilizing response within constraint. Minimize does not mean reducing care; it means reducing distortion. The responder identifies what is essential in the moment—what must be addressed now, what cannot wait, what falls within the limits of available capacity. This narrows the field of action without denying the presence of other needs.

Interpret involves making meaning within constraint. The responder does not wait for full clarity. They work with the clarity available, applying training, protocol, and experience to determine a course of action that is justified within the situation as it is.

Re-engage means continuing forward without requiring that the previous decision be fully resolved. The responder does not remain fixed on what could not be done. They return to the field, carrying the awareness of limitation without allowing it to halt response.

MIR does not resolve scarcity.

It stabilizes movement within it.

The fourth movement is engaging the M.O.R.A.L framework under compression. At the level of meaning, the responder recognizes that the situation is structured by limitation. The field is not disordered. It is constrained. This reorients interpretation from failure to condition.

At the level of obligation, the responder acknowledges that multiple obligations are present and that not all can be fulfilled. Responsibility is real, but not singular. It is distributed across competing demands.

At the level of judgment, the responder evaluates based on priority and impact, not completeness. The question is not whether the response meets every need, but whether it aligns with the best possible outcome within existing limits.

At the level of agency, the responder acts directionally. Action is focused, intentional, and bounded. To act in one place is to not act in another, and this is understood as part of the structure, not a deviation from it.

At the level of legacy, the responder anticipates that these decisions will remain. They are not erased by necessity. They are carried. This anticipation allows for later processing, rather than expecting full resolution in the moment.

The fifth movement is resisting retrospective distortion. After the intensity of response subsides, the individual may return to decisions made under constraint with clarity that was not available at the time. This can create the impression that a different decision should have been made.

Resisting distortion requires returning to the conditions as they were.

What was known?

What was possible?

What constraints were present?

The question is not what would have been ideal.

It is what was actionable.

This prevents hindsight from rewriting the structure of the moment.

The sixth movement is re-engaging these decisions in community. Disaster response is rarely an individual effort. Processing should not be either. Bringing these experiences into conversation allows for shared recognition of constraint, shared interpretation of decisions, and shared integration of what remains unresolved.

The goal is not to remove the weight.

It is to distribute it.

The seventh movement is integrating necessity and loss without collapsing them into one another. Each decision under scarcity contains both elements. There is necessity—the requirement to act within constraint—and there is loss—the presence of needs that were not met.

Integration holds both.

Without allowing necessity to erase loss.

Or loss to negate necessity.

Working under constraint, then, is not about achieving resolution.

It is about maintaining integrity within limitation.

From undifferentiated pressure to structured response.

From assumed failure to recognized constraint.

From isolated decision-making to shared processing.

From accumulation to integration.

The field does not change.

Scarcity remains.

Compression remains.

But the way the responder moves within it does.

The work continues.

And the responder remains able to continue with it.

REFLECTION

When you are working under pressure, how do you interpret what cannot be done?

Do you experience it as failure?

Or as limitation?

What tells you the difference?

When everything feels urgent, how do you determine what is essential?

What guides your prioritization in the moment—training, instinct, available resources, or something else?

How do you carry decisions that were necessary but incomplete?

Do you revisit them?

Set them aside?

Reconstruct them with more information than you had at the time?

What changes when you return to the conditions of the moment as they were, rather than as they appear in hindsight?

What do you assume about what "should have" happened?

And how do those assumptions shape how you evaluate your actions?

How do you experience the presence of competing obligations?

Do you try to resolve them?

Rank them?

Or simply move within them?

What happens when you allow that some obligations could not be fulfilled?

What does that do to your sense of responsibility?

How do you hold the relationship between necessity and loss?

Do you allow both to remain present?

Or does one override the other?

What changes when you name both—clearly, without collapsing them into each other?

When you process these experiences, do you do so alone?

Or with others who understand the structure of the field?

What difference does that make?

What would it mean to remain engaged in this work without requiring that every decision resolve?

WHAT'S AHEAD

We have seen how moral injury emerges in environments of urgency, uncertainty, and consequence.

Next, we will examine healthcare—where responsibility, limitation, and human vulnerability intersect.

Chapter 11

Healthcare

PART 1—PROTOCOL AND PATIENT

It did not begin as a conflict.

It began as a standard case.

The chart was complete. The presenting symptoms aligned with known patterns. The pathway forward was already outlined—assessment, stabilization, intervention, discharge or admission depending on response. Nothing in the initial presentation suggested deviation. The system was ready.

That is how it is designed to function.

Protocols exist to create consistency, reduce variability, and ensure that care is delivered according to established standards. They provide a structure that allows multiple practitioners to operate within a shared framework, reduce uncertainty, and make action possible at scale.

He knew the protocol. He had followed it many times. It worked, and in most cases, it worked well.

He entered the room with this already in place. The patient was alert, responsive, able to communicate. The initial assessment aligned with what the chart indicated. Vital signs, symptoms, and history all pointed in a familiar direction. He moved through the sequence—questions, observations, standard checks.

The structure held.

And then, something did not.

It was not dramatic, not immediately visible. It appeared as a slight misalignment between what the protocol anticipated and what the patient expressed. The symptoms were consistent, but the experience was not fully captured by the available categories. Something remained that did not fit cleanly into the expected pattern.

He paused—not in action, but in interpretation—and continued the assessment with growing awareness that something remained unaccounted for. The protocol continued to guide, but it no longer contained the whole.

This is where the tension begins—not in opposition, but in divergence. The system moves in one direction. The patient presents in another.

He returned to the protocol. That is what training reinforces. When uncertainty arises, return to structure. Follow the sequence. Apply the criteria. Trust the framework.

He did.

He moved through each step, confirming what could be confirmed, documenting what was required, aligning the case with the established pathway.

Everything checked.

Everything aligned.

And still, something remained.

The patient spoke again—this time not in the language of symptoms, but in the language of experience. There was a quality to what was being described that did not fit neatly within the categories of the protocol.

It was not that the protocol was wrong.

It was that it was incomplete.

He recognized the gap—not fully, but enough.

The decision point approached—not as a single moment, but as an accumulation. Each step of the protocol brought him closer to an outcome that, on paper, made sense. The criteria were met. The pathway was clear. But the patient in front of him did not fully align with that outcome.

At the level of action, the next step was obvious.

At the level of judgment, it was not.

He stood within the structure of the system, holding two forms of clarity at once—the protocol indicating one course, the patient suggesting another. Neither could be dismissed. The protocol was not arbitrary; it was built from evidence, accumulated experience, and the need to standardize care across cases. The patient was not abstract. They were present, particular, unrepeatable.

He could follow the protocol.

He could attend to the patient.

He could not fully do both in the same way.

This is where the conflict becomes visible—not as a failure of the system or of the practitioner, but as a condition that emerges when structured care meets particular need.

He considered deviation. That possibility existed. But deviation is not neutral. It carries its own weight—documentation, justification, potential scrutiny, and the need to explain why the established pathway was not followed. The system does not prevent deviation, but it does not make it easy.

He moved forward—not fully within the protocol, not fully outside of it—adjusting, modifying, and attempting to hold both. The decision did not resolve the tension.

It redistributed it.

Part remained with the patient.

Part shifted into the system.

Part stayed with him.

He completed the encounter, documented the case, and moved to the next. From the outside, the sequence appeared intact. The system functioned. The patient received care. The process continued.

But the experience did not close.

It remained—not as uncertainty, but as tension.

He had not failed to act. He had not ignored the protocol. And yet, he could not fully say that the care provided had been entirely aligned with either. He had worked within a space where alignment was not fully possible.

This is where healthcare reveals its deeper structure. It is not only the application of knowledge.

It is the navigation of constraint.

The practitioner is not only diagnosing and treating. He is interpreting, adjusting, and deciding within a system that cannot fully account for every patient it serves.

The protocol did not fail.

The patient did not deviate.

The gap remained.

And in that gap, the work became moral.

PART 2—SYSTEM CONSTRAINT AND ETHICAL CONFLICT

The experience described in the previous section is structured not only by clinical complexity, but by institutional design. The practitioner is not operating in an open field. They are working within a system—one that organizes care through protocols, policies, documentation requirements, resource allocation, and accountability structures.

These elements are not incidental.

They are necessary.

Without them, care becomes inconsistent, unpredictable, and difficult to sustain across large populations. Systems exist to create reliability, reduce variation, and ensure that care can be delivered at scale.

But systems are not neutral.

They shape how care is given.

They determine what can be done, how it can be done, and under what conditions deviation is permitted.

This introduces a distinct pathway within moral injury.

In situations of perpetration, the tension emerges from what one has done. In witnessing, it emerges from what one has seen. In omission, it emerges from what one did not do. In disorientation, it emerges from the instability of meaning. In disaster response, it emerges from constraint under scarcity. In healthcare systems, the tension emerges from the collision between structured care and particular need.

The problem is not lack of knowledge.

It is limitation within structure.

At the level of meaning, system constraint alters how the situation is understood. The practitioner does not encounter the patient in isolation. The patient is encountered within a framework that has already defined pathways, categories, and expected responses. The individual is interpreted through the system.

This does not eliminate the individual.

But it conditions how the individual is seen.

Meaning becomes mediated. The practitioner must hold two forms of understanding at once—the patient as presented and the patient as defined within the system. When these align, care proceeds smoothly.

When they do not, tension emerges.

At the level of obligation, the practitioner experiences competing responsibilities. There is obligation to the patient—to attend, respond, and provide care that reflects particular need. There is also obligation to the system—to follow protocols, document appropriately, and operate within institutional expectations.

Neither obligation is optional.

Both are real.

But they are not always compatible.

This produces a distinct tension—not between right and wrong, but between two legitimate claims on action. The practitioner is not choosing whether to act.

They are choosing which obligation to prioritize.

At the level of judgment, the practitioner must evaluate not only what is clinically appropriate, but what is institutionally permissible. Decisions are made within overlapping frameworks—clinical knowledge, professional standards, and system constraints.

The question is no longer only:

What does this patient need?

It becomes:

What can be done for this patient within the limits of the system?

This shift is subtle.

But it reconfigures decision-making.

The practitioner is not only applying knowledge.

They are negotiating boundaries.

At the level of agency, the practitioner remains active, but action is shaped by the system in which it occurs. They can act—but not without reference to protocols, policies, and governing expectations. Agency becomes conditional—not absent, but mediated.

The practitioner can choose.

But not without consequence.

Deviation from protocol may require justification, invite scrutiny, and carry professional risk. Even when clinically appropriate, it is not neutral. This constrains action—not by removing options, but by attaching weight to them.

At the level of legacy, the effects of system constraint extend beyond the moment of care. Decisions made within these structures persist. The practitioner may revisit them not only in terms of clinical outcome, but in terms of alignment—whether the care reflected the patient, the protocol, or a negotiated position between the two.

These moments accumulate—not as isolated events, but as patterns. The practitioner begins to recognize that this tension is not occasional.

It is structural.

This is where ethical conflict becomes visible.

Ethical conflict in this context does not arise from uncertainty about what is right. Often, the practitioner knows what would best serve the patient. The conflict arises from the inability to act fully on that knowledge within the constraints of the system.

The issue is not ambiguity.

It is restriction.

At the level of experience, this produces a specific form of strain. The practitioner is required to act in ways that are justified within the system, but that may feel incomplete in relation to the patient. The decision may be defensible—even correct within institutional standards—and still leave something unresolved.

This is not error.

It is not negligence.

It is the experience of working within limits that prevent full alignment between knowledge and action.

At the level of meaning, ethical conflict disrupts coherence. The practitioner holds an understanding of what care requires and an awareness of what the system allows. These do not always converge.

Meaning does not collapse.

But it divides.

At the level of obligation, the practitioner cannot fully satisfy both claims. To adhere strictly to protocol may produce care that feels insufficiently responsive to the patient. To prioritize the patient fully may require deviation from the system.

Either path carries cost.

At the level of judgment, the practitioner must decide which cost to bear. This decision is not resolved by clinical knowledge alone. It requires weighing competing goods—consistency and flexibility, standardization and responsiveness, institutional integrity and individual care.

At the level of agency, action becomes negotiated. The practitioner moves within the system, adjusting where possible, bending where permitted, holding as much alignment as can be maintained.

But full alignment is not always available.

At the level of legacy, these decisions remain. They are carried not only as clinical cases, but as moral experiences. The practitioner remembers not only what was done, but what could not be done.

System constraint does not eliminate ethical responsibility.

It reframes it.

It requires the practitioner to act within a structure that both enables and limits care, to navigate competing obligations that cannot always be reconciled, and to carry the residual presence of what could not be fully aligned.

The tension is not that the practitioner does not care.

It is that care itself is constrained.

And within that constraint, every decision carries both justification and remainder.

PART 3—CLINICAL DECISION WITH MORAL WEIGHT

The decision did not arrive as a single moment.

It formed gradually.

He had already completed the initial assessment. The protocol had been followed, the criteria applied, the pathway identified. From the standpoint of the system, the case was clear. The documentation aligned. The indicators pointed in a consistent direction.

The next step was already defined.

But the patient remained.

Not as data.

Not as a category.

As a person whose experience did not fully resolve within the structure that had been applied.

He returned to the bedside—not to repeat the assessment, but to listen again. The patient's condition had not changed in a measurable way. Vital signs remained stable. The presenting symptoms were consistent.

And yet, something in the account continued to resist closure.

At the level of meaning, the situation was no longer defined solely by what could be measured. The protocol captured what was visible, but not everything that was present. The patient described a pattern—subtle, difficult to quantify, but persistent. It did not contradict the clinical findings.

It exceeded them.

He held both—the clarity of the system and the ambiguity of the patient's experience.

They did not align.

At the level of obligation, the tension sharpened. He was responsible to the patient—to attend to what was being expressed, even if it could not be fully substantiated within the framework of the protocol. He was also responsible to the system—to act in accordance with established standards, avoid unnecessary intervention, and use resources appropriately.

Neither obligation could be dismissed.

Both demanded response.

But they did not lead to the same action.

At the level of judgment, he evaluated the options. Following the protocol would produce a course of care that was justified, efficient, and aligned with institutional expectations. It would also leave the patient's expressed concern partially unaddressed.

Deviating from the protocol would allow further exploration—additional testing, extended observation, a different pathway of care. It would also require justification, consume additional resources, and move outside the standard sequence.

Both paths were defensible.

Neither was complete.

This is where ethical conflict becomes fully visible—not as uncertainty about what is right, but as the presence of two valid courses of action that cannot be fully reconciled.

At the level of agency, he acted—not entirely within the protocol, not entirely outside of it. He adjusted, extending the evaluation beyond what was strictly required, but not to the point of abandoning the structure that guided the case. He documented carefully, noting the reasons for deviation and aligning his decision as closely as possible with the language of the system.

The action did not resolve the tension.

It redistributed it.

Part remained in the patient's condition.

Part shifted into the system.

Part stayed with him.

He continued the encounter, moving through the adjusted plan of care. The additional steps did not immediately produce clarity. Findings remained inconclusive. The patient's experience remained only partially captured.

From the outside, the case remained stable.

From within, it did not settle.

At the level of outcome, the situation progressed. The patient was either admitted for further observation or discharged with follow-up, depending on how the balance was ultimately held. The system absorbed the decision. The documentation supported it. The sequence continued.

But the experience did not close.

At the level of retrospective meaning, he revisited the decision—not as a question of correctness, but of alignment. He could see the structure clearly—the protocol, the divergence, the adjustment, the outcome.

The reasoning held.

And yet, something remained unresolved.

He had not ignored the patient.

He had not disregarded the system.

And still, he could not say that the two had been fully reconciled.

At the level of retrospective obligation, the tension persisted. He had responded to both claims, but not fully satisfied either. The patient's experience had been acknowledged, but not fully explained. The system had been followed, but not without modification.

The obligations had been held.

Not resolved.

At the level of retrospective judgment, he evaluated the decision again. He could justify the adjustment. He could defend the documentation. He could align the action with both clinical reasoning and institutional expectations.

The decision was sound.

But it was not complete.

At the level of retrospective agency, there was no alternative that removed the tension. A stricter adherence to protocol would reduce system deviation but increase patient misalignment. A fuller departure from the protocol would honor the patient more completely but at greater institutional cost.

There was no version of the moment in which both were fully satisfied.

The structure did not allow it.

At the level of legacy, the experience did not remain isolated. It became part of a pattern—one of many cases in which system and patient did not fully align. Each instance reinforced the recognition that this tension was not exceptional.

It was embedded.

He began to understand that clinical practice is not only the application of knowledge within a system.

It is the navigation of the space between them.

The practitioner is not only diagnosing and treating.

He is interpreting, adjusting, and deciding within limits that cannot always be reconciled.

The protocol did not fail.

The patient did not deviate.

The gap remained.

And in that gap, the decision carried weight.

Not because it was wrong.

But because it could not be complete.

PART 4—NAVIGATING INSTITUTIONAL LIMITS: MIR + M.O.R.A.L IN PRACTICE

When care takes place within structured systems, the instinct is to resolve tension by choosing one side fully—either strict adherence to protocol or full prioritization of the patient. The pressure to simplify is strong. Systems reward consistency. Patients require responsiveness.

But practice resists that simplicity.

The task is not to eliminate the tension. It is to navigate it with clarity. What is not processed in the moment does not disappear. It accumulates.

The first movement is recognition. Recognition names the condition accurately. The practitioner is not failing to care. The practitioner is working within a system that both enables and limits what care can be. This distinction is essential: it is not that I did not respond; it is that full alignment was not available. Recognition interrupts the tendency to interpret tension as personal failure and locates the experience within the structure of healthcare, allowing the practitioner to remain engaged without misidentifying the nature of the work.

The second movement is differentiating between system necessity and patient particularity. Protocols exist for valid reasons—they create reliability, reduce error, and allow care to be delivered across contexts. Patient need, however, is particular and does not always conform to standardized pathways. The practitioner must hold both—not as competing errors, but as competing goods. The tension is not between right and wrong.

It is between two legitimate claims.

The third movement is applying MIR within institutional constraint. MIR—Minimize, Interpret, Re-engage—stabilizes action without collapsing tension. Minimize reduces distortion by identifying what is essential in the moment—what must be addressed now, what falls within safe and appropriate care, and what cannot be fully resolved within the current structure. This clarifies the field without denying complexity. Interpret makes meaning within constraint. The practitioner does not wait for full alignment between protocol and patient, but works with the alignment that is available, drawing on clinical judgment, experience, and ethical reasoning to determine a course of action justified within existing conditions. Re-engage continues the work without requiring that the tension be resolved, carrying awareness forward without allowing it to halt care.

MIR does not remove institutional limits.

It stabilizes practice within them.

The fourth movement is engaging the M.O.R.A.L framework within systems. At the level of meaning, the practitioner recognizes that care is mediated through structure; the patient is encountered both directly and through the system. This dual awareness prevents over-identification with either protocol or individual. At the level of obligation, the practitioner acknowledges multiple responsibilities—to the patient, to professional standards, and to institutional expectations—none of which can always be fully reconciled. At the level of judgment, the practitioner evaluates based on alignment rather than perfection; the question is not whether the decision resolves all tension, but whether it holds the best possible balance within existing limits. At the level of agency, the practitioner acts within constraint—adjusting where possible, documenting where necessary, and accepting that action carries consequence. Agency is not removed.

It is conditioned.

At the level of legacy, the practitioner anticipates that these moments will remain. They are not erased by justification. They are carried, allowing for later reflection without requiring full resolution in the moment.

The fifth movement is resisting retrospective simplification. After the encounter, there is a tendency to reconstruct the decision with clarity that was not available at the time. The practitioner may feel that a clearer path should have been taken. Resisting simplification requires returning to the conditions as they were—what was known, what was permitted, and what constraints were present. The question is not what would have been ideal.

It is what could be done.

This prevents hindsight from collapsing complexity into false clarity.

The sixth movement is re-engaging these experiences in community. Healthcare is not practiced in isolation, and processing should not be either. Ethics consultations, peer discussion, and interdisciplinary reflection provide space to revisit decisions with others who understand the structure. The goal is not agreement.

It is shared holding.

The weight is not removed.

It is distributed.

The seventh movement is integrating tension without collapsing care. The practitioner learns to hold both system and patient without allowing one to erase the other. Protocol remains. Particularity remains. Integration does not resolve the gap.

It makes it livable.

Working within institutional limits is not about achieving perfect alignment. It is about sustaining integrity within constraint—moving from assumed failure to recognized structure, from forced resolution to held tension, from isolated judgment to shared interpretation, from accumulation to integration.

The system does not disappear.

The patient does not disappear.

The gap remains.

But the practitioner learns to stand within it.

And continue.

REFLECTION

When you work within structured systems, how do you experience the relationship between protocol and person?

Do you experience them as aligned?

Or as something you must constantly negotiate?

When they diverge, what do you feel first?

Clarity?

Pressure?

Tension?

What tells you which direction to move?

What do you trust in those moments—training, instinct, experience, policy?

How do you decide when to remain within the structure?

And when to adjust it?

What do you assume about deviation?

Is it risk?

Responsibility?

Failure?

Care?

How do those assumptions shape your decisions?

When you follow the protocol and something remains unresolved, how do you carry that?

Do you name it?

Set it aside?

Return to it later?

When you adjust beyond the protocol, how do you hold the weight of that decision?

Do you justify it?

Defend it?

Question it?

What changes when you return to the conditions as they were, rather than as they appear in hindsight?

What do you remember differently?

How do you experience competing obligations—to the patient, to the system, to your role?

Do you try to resolve them?

Balance them?

Or move within them?

What happens when you accept that they cannot always be fully reconciled?

What does that do to your sense of responsibility?

How do you carry the accumulation of these moments?

Do they remain isolated?

Or do they begin to form a pattern?

Where do you process that pattern?

Alone?

With colleagues?

Within a system that recognizes it?

What difference does that make?

What would it mean to continue this work without requiring that protocol and person always fully align?

What would it require to remain present in both—without losing either?

WHAT'S AHEAD

We have seen how moral injury develops within systems of care and constraint.

Next, we will turn to ministry and faith leadership—where moral responsibility is both personal and communal.

Chapter 12

Ministry and Faith Leadership

PART 1—PASTORAL CARE AND INSTITUTIONAL EXPECTATION

It did not begin as a crisis.

It began as a conversation.

The setting was familiar. The rhythms of ministry had already shaped the space—scheduled meetings, pastoral visits, administrative responsibilities, the ongoing life of a community that required both presence and structure. Nothing in the moment suggested it would become something more, and yet the conditions were already there.

He listened.

That is where pastoral work begins—not with solutions or decisions, but with attention. The person across from him spoke slowly, not because the story was unclear, but because it was difficult to say. Details emerged in fragments—experience, emotion, confusion, a sense that something had shifted but could not yet be fully named. He did not interrupt or move too quickly to interpretation. He allowed the account to unfold.

At the level of care, this is what is required: to remain with the person as they speak, to receive what is offered without immediately organizing it into categories or responses. But the context did not remain limited to the moment.

It expanded.

What was being described did not exist in isolation. It touched other relationships, other roles, other parts of the community. The concern did not remain personal.

It became structural.

He began to recognize the implications—not fully, not immediately, but enough to understand that what was being shared would not remain contained within the boundaries of pastoral conversation. There would be consequences—not only for the individual, but for the institution.

This is where the tension begins—not in opposition, but in overlap. Pastoral care and institutional responsibility do not exist in separate domains. They are held within the same role. The pastor is not only present to the person; he is accountable to the community.

He holds both.

And in some moments, they do not align.

He continued to listen, but the nature of the listening changed. It was no longer only receptive. It became interpretive. He began to consider what would be required beyond the conversation—who might need to be involved, what processes might be activated, what responsibilities would emerge.

The care remained.

But it was no longer simple.

At the level of meaning, the situation shifted. The conversation was no longer only about the experience being described, but about what that experience meant within the life of the community. The individual's story carried implications that extended beyond the individual.

Meaning expanded.

And with it, responsibility.

At the level of obligation, the tension sharpened. He was responsible to the person in front of him—to offer care that was attentive, compassionate, and responsive to what was being shared. He was also responsible to the institution—to ensure that the community was protected, that appropriate structures were followed, and that the integrity of the system was maintained.

Neither obligation could be set aside.

Both were real.

But they did not lead to the same action.

Pastoral care called for presence, confidentiality, and trust. Institutional expectation called for process, disclosure, and accountability. He could not fully do both in the same way.

This is where the conflict becomes visible—not as a failure of care or leadership, but as a condition that emerges when relational trust meets institutional responsibility.

He did not move immediately to decision. He remained in the conversation. That, too, is part of the work—to stay long enough to understand what is being asked, not only by the person, but by the situation.

The person finished speaking.

Silence followed—not empty, but full.

He held it.

Within that silence, the next movement began to form—not as clarity, but as awareness. Whatever he said next would not remain within the room. It would shape what followed.

He could respond pastorally—holding the conversation within the bounds of care, allowing trust to remain intact, limiting the immediate expansion of the situation. He could respond institutionally—initiating processes that would move the concern beyond the conversation, involving others, and activating structures designed to address what had been described.

Both responses were valid.

Neither was complete.

At the level of judgment, he began to weigh these paths—not as abstract options, but as real consequences. To remain fully within pastoral care risked leaving the institution unaddressed. To move fully into institutional response risked altering the trust that had made the conversation possible.

He could not preserve both fully.

Not in the same way.

This is where ministry reveals its deeper structure. It is not only the care of souls.

It is the navigation of roles.

The pastor is not only a caregiver. He is a leader within a system. And the system does not disappear in moments of care.

It intensifies.

He spoke—not to resolve the situation, but to begin to move within it. His words were careful, not because he lacked clarity, but because clarity itself was layered. He acknowledged what had been shared, affirmed its significance, and did not dismiss the experience.

He also did not promise that it would remain contained.

The conversation shifted. The person heard not only care, but implication. Trust remained.

But it changed.

At the level of agency, he acted—not by choosing one role over the other, but by attempting to hold both. He began to move toward institutional response while maintaining as much relational integrity as possible. He did not abandon the pastoral relationship, but he did not remain solely within it.

The decision did not resolve the tension.

It redistributed it.

Part remained with the individual.

Part moved into the institution.

Part stayed with him.

He left the conversation with a sense that something had begun that would not easily end. The decision would extend beyond the moment—into meetings, processes, and further conversations that would require both care and accountability.

From the outside, this is what leadership looks like.

From within, it is something else.

It is the experience of holding responsibilities that cannot always be reconciled.

At the level of legacy, the moment did not close. It became a reference point—not only for what had been done, but for how decisions are made when roles converge. He would return to it—not to question whether he had acted, but to consider how the action had held both care and structure.

He had not failed the person.

He had not failed the institution.

And still, he could not say that both had been fully satisfied.

This is where ministry becomes more than presence.

It becomes burden.

Not because the work is unclear.

But because it is layered.

The pastor is asked to care.

The pastor is asked to lead.

And sometimes, those are not the same.

The roles did not fail.
The person did not deviate.
The institution did not disappear.
The tension remained.
And in that tension, the work became moral.

PART 2—ROLE CONFLICT AND SPIRITUAL BURDEN

The experience described in the previous section is structured not only by relational complexity, but by the nature of the role itself. Ministry is not a single function. It is a convergence of responsibilities—pastoral, institutional, relational, and often theological—held within the same person. These are not separate domains engaged one at a time.

They are simultaneous.

This is what gives the role its depth.

And its strain.

The pastor does not move between identities.

He carries them at once.

This introduces a distinct pathway within moral injury. In situations of perpetration, the tension emerges from what one has done. In witnessing, it emerges from what one has seen. In omission, it emerges from what one did not do. In disorientation, it emerges from the instability of meaning. In disaster response, it emerges from constraint under scarcity. In healthcare, it emerges from structured systems.

In ministry, the tension emerges from role convergence.

The problem is not confusion about the role.

It is conflict within it.

At the level of meaning, role conflict alters how the situation is understood. The pastor encounters the same event through multiple lenses at once. As a caregiver, the focus remains on the person—their experience, vulnerability, and need for presence. As a leader, the focus expands to the community—its implications, patterns, and responsibilities.

These interpretations do not replace one another.

They coexist.

When they align, the work feels coherent.

When they do not, meaning becomes layered—not unclear, but divided.

At the level of obligation, the pastor experiences competing responsibilities that are equally valid. There is obligation to the individual—to provide care that is attentive, trustworthy, and responsive. There is obligation to the community—to ensure safety, integrity, and accountability. There is often obligation to broader structures—denominational expectations, policies, and ethical standards that guide practice.

None of these obligations can be dismissed.

All carry weight.

But they cannot always be fulfilled in the same way.

This produces a distinct tension—not between right and wrong, but between responsibilities that cannot be simultaneously satisfied.

At the level of judgment, the pastor must determine how to act within this convergence. Decisions are not made within a single framework, but across multiple ones—pastoral, institutional, and theological. The question is not only what is appropriate for the person or required by the system.

It becomes:

What action holds the most integrity across these roles, given that full alignment is not possible?

This question cannot be resolved through rule alone.

It requires discernment.

At the level of agency, the pastor remains active, but action is shaped by the convergence of roles. He can act—but not without affecting each dimension of responsibility. To move toward pastoral care may limit institutional response. To move toward institutional accountability may alter the pastoral relationship.

Agency is not removed.

It is distributed.

Each action carries implications across domains.

At the level of legacy, the effects of role conflict extend beyond the moment of decision. The pastor may revisit these moments not only as choices made, but as expressions of identity—how the role was inhabited, which responsibilities were emphasized, and how the tension was held.

These experiences accumulate—not as isolated events, but as patterns of leadership. The pastor begins to recognize that this tension is not occasional.

It is structural.

This is where spiritual burden becomes visible. Spiritual burden in this context is not simply emotional strain.

It is the weight of carrying responsibility across domains that cannot be fully reconciled.

The pastor is not only managing outcomes.

He is holding meaning.

At the level of experience, this burden takes a particular form. The pastor remains present to the person, aware of institutional implications, and conscious of ethical and theological dimensions—all at once. There is no point at which the role can be reduced to a single function.

The weight is cumulative—not because the pastor is uncertain, but because clarity itself is layered.

At the level of meaning, spiritual burden intensifies the division within interpretation. The pastor may understand what care requires, what leadership requires, and what faithfulness requires—and recognize that these do not fully converge.

Meaning does not disappear.

It multiplies.

At the level of obligation, the burden is not that responsibility is unclear, but that it is abundant. The pastor is accountable in multiple directions, each legitimate and each demanding response.

To act is to respond.

And to not respond elsewhere.

At the level of judgment, decisions carry not only practical consequence, but spiritual weight. The pastor is not only asking what is effective or appropriate.

He is asking what is faithful.

This introduces a dimension that cannot be resolved through policy or protocol alone.

At the level of agency, action is taken with the awareness that no choice will fully resolve the tension. The pastor acts, not because the path is free of cost, but because action is required within conditions where cost is unavoidable.

Agency becomes faithful movement within limitation.

At the level of legacy, these moments remain as part of the pastor's understanding of vocation. They shape not only future decisions, but the sense of what it means to carry the role itself.

Spiritual burden is not an interruption of ministry.

It is part of it.

Role conflict does not indicate a failure of leadership.

It reveals its complexity.

It requires the pastor to inhabit a role that holds multiple legitimate claims without expecting they can always be reconciled, to act within that tension, and to carry the weight of decisions that reflect both care and consequence.

The tension is not that the pastor does not know what to do.

It is that no single action can fully satisfy what is known.

And within that reality, the work becomes not only practical.

But spiritual.

PART 3—LEADERSHIP DECISION WITH MORAL CONSEQUENCE

The decision did not arrive all at once.

It unfolded.

The conversation in his office did not remain contained there. What had been spoken could not be unheard, and what had been entrusted could not be treated as if it carried no further implication. He left the meeting aware that the situation had already begun to move beyond the boundaries of pastoral care—not visibly, but structurally.

At first, the work remained relational. He checked in, followed up, and maintained the connection that had made the initial conversation possible. The pastoral role continued—present, attentive, responsive.

But the awareness did not recede.

It sharpened.

What had been shared was not only personal. It carried implications for others within the community, suggested patterns that might extend beyond a single interaction, and raised the possibility that the issue was not isolated.

At the level of meaning, the situation shifted again. The story was no longer only the story of one person. It became a question about the life of the community—its safety, its structures, its integrity. The pastor could no longer interpret the situation through a single lens.

He had to hold both—the particular and the collective.

They did not align.

At the level of obligation, the tension intensified. He was responsible to the individual—to honor what had been shared, maintain trust, and provide care that did not expose the person unnecessarily. He was also responsible to the community—to ensure that potential harm was addressed, that appropriate processes were followed, and that the well-being of others was considered.

Neither obligation diminished.

Both expanded.

And they did not lead to the same action.

At the level of judgment, he began to consider what movement would be required. Remaining fully within pastoral care would preserve the relationship but risk leaving broader implications unaddressed. Initiating institutional response would engage necessary structures but alter the relational dynamic that had made the disclosure possible.

Both paths carried consequence.

Neither removed the tension.

This is where the decision began to take shape—not as a clear answer, but as a narrowing of what could be held. The situation did not allow indefinite delay. To do nothing was itself a decision.

And it carried weight.

At the level of agency, he acted—not abruptly and not without care, but decisively enough to move the situation beyond the private space of pastoral conversation. He contacted those who needed to be involved and began the process the institution required. He documented what had been shared—not as a betrayal of trust, but as acknowledgment that the situation had implications beyond the individual.

The action did not resolve the tension.

It redistributed it.

Part remained with the person who had trusted him.

Part moved into the system.

Part stayed with him.

The response began to unfold—meetings, conversations, procedures that introduced new voices into what had been a private exchange. The situation became visible, structured, and subject to processes designed to address exactly this kind of concern.

From the outside, this is what responsible leadership looks like.

From within, it is more complex.

At the level of experience, he remained aware of what had shifted. The relationship with the individual changed—not necessarily broken, but altered. Trust was no longer held in the same way. It had expanded into something else—shared, distributed, no longer contained within the original conversation.

He had not intended to diminish that trust.

But he could not preserve it unchanged.

At the level of outcome, the process moved forward. The institution responded. Actions were taken. The situation was addressed within established structures.

From a procedural standpoint, the response was appropriate.

From a relational standpoint, something remained.

At the level of retrospective meaning, he revisited the decision—not as a question of whether action was required, but of how that action had held both care and responsibility. He could see the sequence clearly—the conversation, the recognition, the movement toward institutional response, the unfolding of process.

The logic held.

The necessity was clear.

And yet, something did not fully resolve.

He had honored the responsibility to the community.

He had not abandoned the individual.

And still, he could not say that both had been fully satisfied.

At the level of retrospective obligation, the tension persisted. He had acted in accordance with both roles, but the experience of holding them did not collapse into a single sense of completion. The individual's trust had been transformed. The institution's response had been activated.

The obligations had been engaged.

Not reconciled.

At the level of retrospective judgment, he evaluated the decision again. He could justify the movement toward institutional process, articulate the reasons clearly, and align the decision with ethical responsibility, denominational expectation, and the need to protect the community.

The decision was sound.

But it was not complete.

At the level of retrospective agency, there was no alternative that removed the tension. To remain fully within pastoral care would have preserved the relationship more completely but risked leaving broader concerns unaddressed. To move more quickly or more forcefully into institutional response would have strengthened accountability but further altered the relational trust.

There was no version of the moment in which both were fully preserved.

The structure did not allow it.

At the level of legacy, the experience did not remain isolated. It became part of his understanding of leadership—not as a series of clear decisions, but as the ongoing navigation of roles that cannot always be aligned. He recognized that this was not an exceptional case.

It was representative.

The work of ministry would continue to present moments where care and responsibility converge without resolution. He was not only remembering the decision.

He was recognizing the pattern.

This is where ministry reveals its deeper demand. It is not only the presence of care, and not only the exercise of leadership.

It is the holding of both.

The pastor is not only a caregiver. He is not only an institutional leader.

He is the one who must act where those roles meet.

The decision did not fail.

The relationship did not disappear.

The institution did not overtake the moment.

The tension remained.

And in that tension, the decision carried consequence.

Not because it was wrong.

But because it could not be complete.

PART 4—HOLDING TENSION IN MINISTRY: MIR + M.O.R.A.L IN PRACTICE

When pastoral care and institutional responsibility converge, the instinct is to resolve the tension by privileging one over the other—to remain fully within the pastoral relationship or to move decisively into institutional process. The pressure to simplify is strong. Care calls for trust. Leadership calls for accountability.

But ministry resists that separation.

The task is not to eliminate the tension.

It is to hold it with integrity.

What is not processed in the moment does not disappear.

It accumulates.

The first movement is recognition. Recognition names the condition accurately. The pastor is not failing to care. The pastor is not failing to lead. The pastor is working within a role that requires both, even when they cannot be fully aligned. This distinction is essential: it is not that I chose wrong; it is that full alignment was not available. Recognition interrupts the tendency to interpret tension as failure and locates the experience within the nature of ministry, allowing the pastor to remain engaged without misidentifying the work.

The second movement is differentiating between relational trust and institutional responsibility. Pastoral care is grounded in presence, confidentiality, and trust. Institutional leadership is grounded in accountability, process, and the well-being of the community. Both are necessary. Both are good. But they are not the same. The pastor must hold both—not as competing errors, but as competing goods. The tension is not between care and harm.

It is between care and responsibility.

The third movement is applying MIR within ministry. MIR—Minimize, Interpret, Re-engage—stabilizes action without collapsing tension. Minimize reduces distortion by identifying what is essential in the moment—what must be held relationally, what cannot be ignored institutionally, and what cannot be fully resolved within the current situation. This clarifies the field without denying complexity. Interpret makes meaning within convergence. The pastor does not wait for full clarity between roles, but works with the clarity that is available, drawing on theological reflection, pastoral experience, and ethical discernment to determine a course of action that holds integrity across domains. Re-engage continues the work without requiring that the tension be resolved, carrying awareness forward without allowing it to halt ministry.

MIR does not remove role conflict.

It stabilizes presence within it.

The fourth movement is engaging the M.O.R.A.L framework within ministry. At the level of meaning, the pastor recognizes that situations are interpreted through multiple lenses—pastoral, institutional, and theological. This prevents reduction to a single dimension. At the level of obligation, the pastor acknowledges multiple responsibilities—to the individual, the community, and the broader structures that shape the life of the church—none of which can always be reconciled. At the level of judgment, the pastor evaluates based on faithfulness rather than resolution; the question is not whether the decision satisfies every demand, but whether it reflects integrity across roles within existing limits. At the level of agency, the pastor acts within convergence—aware that every decision affects multiple domains. Action is taken not because it removes tension, but because it responds to it faithfully.

Agency is not simplified.

It is deepened.

At the level of legacy, the pastor anticipates that these moments will remain. They are not erased by explanation or justification. They are carried, becoming part of the ongoing experience of ministry and shaping the understanding of vocation itself.

The fifth movement is resisting retrospective spiritual distortion. After the moment, there is a tendency to interpret the decision through a simplified theological lens—to name one action as fully faithful and another as less so without returning to the complexity of the situation as it was. Resisting distortion requires returning to the conditions as they were—what was known, what responsibilities were present, and what could be held. The question is not what would have been ideal.

It is what was faithful within limitation.

This prevents reflection from collapsing complexity into false clarity.

The sixth movement is re-engaging these experiences in community. Ministry is not an individual vocation; it is held within a body. Processing these moments with trusted colleagues, supervisors, or spiritual directors allows for shared discernment. The goal is not resolution.

It is faithful holding.

The weight is not removed.

It is shared.

The seventh movement is integrating care and responsibility without collapsing either. The pastor learns to hold relational trust and institutional accountability without allowing one to erase the other. Care remains. Responsibility remains.

Integration does not resolve the gap.

It makes it inhabitable.

Working within ministry is not about achieving perfect alignment between roles. It is about sustaining faithfulness within their convergence—moving from assumed failure to recognized vocation, from forced resolution to faithful tension, from isolated discernment to shared wisdom, from accumulation to integration.

The role does not divide.
The responsibilities do not disappear.
The tension remains.
But the pastor learns to stand within it.
And continue.

REFLECTION

When you think about your role in ministry, how do you understand it?

As singular?

Or as layered?

When pastoral care and institutional responsibility converge, what do you experience first?

Clarity?

Pressure?

Weight?

How do you interpret that experience?

As failure?

As complexity?

As calling?

When you are with someone in need, what do you feel most responsible for?

Their care?

Their trust?

Their outcome?

What happens when that responsibility expands beyond the individual?

How do you respond when a pastoral conversation begins to carry institutional consequence?

What changes in you?

What do you begin to hold?

How do you understand trust in those moments?

Is it something to be preserved?

Something to be shared?

Something that inevitably changes?

How do those assumptions shape your decisions?

When you act in ways that alter a pastoral relationship, how do you carry that?

Do you justify it?

Grieve it?

Revisit it?

How do you understand faithfulness in these moments?

As alignment?

As outcome?

As something else?

When you look back, what do you notice?

Do you see clarity that was not available at the time?

Do you hold yourself to that clarity?

What changes when you return to the conditions as they were?

What was known?

What was required?

What could be held?

How do you experience the weight of holding multiple responsibilities at once?

Do you try to resolve them?

Balance them?

Or move within them?

Where do you process that weight?

Alone?

With colleagues?

With those who understand the role?

What difference does that make?

What patterns do you begin to see in your decisions?

What do they reveal about how you inhabit your role?

What would it mean to continue in ministry without requiring that care and responsibility always fully align?

What would it require to remain present in both—without losing either?

WHAT'S NEXT

We have seen how moral injury shapes those who are called to guide, care, and remain.

Next, we will consider public life and leadership—where decisions carry wide and lasting consequence.

Chapter 13

Public Life and Leadership

PART 1—POLICY AND PEOPLE

It did not begin as a crisis.

It began as a briefing.

The room was structured for clarity—reports prepared, data organized, projections outlined in measured language. The issue had been identified, the parameters defined, and the possible responses mapped. There was a sense that the situation, while complex, could be managed within the existing framework. That is how public leadership often begins—with information, structure, and the expectation that decisions can be made by weighing options and selecting the most effective course of action.

He listened.

Not only to what was being said, but to how it was being framed. The language was precise—metrics, timelines, resource allocation, projected impact—each element presented in a way that allowed the situation to be understood within the logic of policy.

The system was speaking.

And it was coherent.

The recommendations followed. Options were outlined with corresponding risks and benefits, their implications described in terms that could be compared, measured, and evaluated. This is how policy operates: it translates complexity into form, creates pathways for action, and enables decisions to be made at scale. He had worked within this structure before and understood its necessity. Without it, leadership becomes reactive and inconsistent, unable to sustain response across large systems. Policy provides continuity, creates order, and allows institutions to function.

But policy does not encounter people directly.

It encounters them through representation.

Through data.

Through abstraction.

The briefing concluded, and the room shifted. What had been presented as structure now required decision. He reviewed the options again—not for information, but for consequence. Each path was viable within the logic of policy. Each could be justified. Each aligned with certain priorities and constraints.

And each would affect people—not in aggregate, but in particular.

He knew that. Even as the discussion remained at the level of policy, he could see what was not fully present in the room. The individuals who would be affected were represented in numbers, categories, and projections.

But they were not here.

This is where the tension begins—not in opposition, but in translation. Policy organizes reality in a way that makes action possible. People experience reality in ways that cannot be fully contained within that organization.

The two do not always align.

He asked questions—not to challenge the data, but to understand its limits: What was assumed? What was not captured? What would be affected that could not be easily measured? The answers were sufficient, but not complete. They could not be. That is not a failure of policy.

It is a condition of it.

At the level of meaning, the situation divided. Within the framework of policy, the decision could be understood as effective, efficient, and aligned with institutional goals. Outside that framework, the same decision would be experienced differently—by individuals whose lives would be shaped by outcomes that could not be fully anticipated.

He held both—the clarity of the system and the reality of those not present within it.

They did not align.

At the level of obligation, the tension sharpened. He was responsible to the system—to act in ways consistent with policy, preserve institutional integrity, and sustain coordinated response. He was also responsible to the people affected—to consider impact not only as outcome, but as lived experience.

Neither obligation could be set aside.

Both were real.

But they did not lead to the same decision.

Policy called for consistency.

People required responsiveness.

He could not fully do both in the same way.

This is where the conflict becomes visible—not as a failure of leadership or policy, but as a condition that emerges when systems designed for scale encounter lives that cannot be scaled.

He returned to the options. Each remained defensible. Each carried cost—not only in measurable outcomes, but in lived consequence. He considered the language of justification—the explanations that would accompany the decision, the ways it would be communicated, and the rationale offered to those who would ask why this path had been chosen.

The justification would hold.

It would be clear.

It would be grounded in data, process, and responsibility.

And still, it would not contain everything.

He knew that.

The decision approached—not as certainty, but as commitment. To choose was to move forward within the structure of policy, knowing the effects would extend beyond it.

He spoke—not to resolve the tension, but to act within it. The decision aligned with the framework that had been presented. It followed the logic of the system. It could be implemented, communicated, and sustained.

It made sense.

And it carried weight.

Part of that weight remained within the policy—its constraints, assumptions, and limitations. Part moved into the lives of those affected. Part stayed with him.

The meeting concluded. From the outside, the process had functioned as intended—information gathered, options evaluated, decision made. From within, the experience did not close.

He could see the outcome clearly.

He could defend the decision.

He could explain it.

And still, something remained.

He had not ignored the people.

He had not disregarded the policy.

And yet, he could not say that both had been fully held.

This is where public leadership reveals its deeper structure. It is not only the application of policy.

It is the navigation of consequence.

The leader is not only deciding between options. He is acting within a system that requires abstraction, while knowing that what is affected cannot be fully abstracted.

The policy did not fail.

The people did not disappear.

The gap remained.

And in that gap, the work became moral.

PART 2—COMPROMISE, RESPONSIBILITY, AND MORAL COST

The experience described in the previous section is shaped not only by the complexity of information, but by the nature of decision-making within public systems. Leadership at this level does not operate in isolated moments of clarity. It operates within conditions where multiple legitimate goods must be weighed, prioritized, and enacted across populations.

This is where compromise becomes unavoidable.

Compromise, in this context, is not a failure of conviction.

It is a function of scale.

Policy decisions are rarely between right and wrong. More often, they involve competing goods—efficiency and equity, stability and responsiveness, short-term impact and long-term consequence. Each carries justification. Each represents a form of responsibility.

But they cannot always be fully held together.

At the level of meaning, compromise reshapes how decisions are understood. The leader does not encounter a single narrative, but multiple interpretations shaped by differing priorities, values, and perspectives. Within the system, a decision may be framed as necessary, effective, or responsible. Outside of it, the same decision may be experienced as insufficient, harmful, or incomplete.

Meaning does not collapse.

It diverges.

The leader must hold both—how the decision functions within the system, and how it will be experienced beyond it.

At the level of obligation, responsibility expands rather than resolves. The leader is accountable to the system—to maintain continuity, act within established structures, and ensure decisions can be implemented and sustained. The leader is also accountable to those affected—to consider not only aggregate outcomes, but lived consequences.

These obligations are not hierarchical.

They are simultaneous.

And they are not always compatible.

This produces a specific form of tension—not between right and wrong, but between responsibilities that cannot be fully satisfied at once.

At the level of judgment, compromise becomes selection within limitation. The leader must determine which goods can be most fully held, which costs can be borne, and which consequences must be accepted. This is not a question of eliminating harm.

It is a question of distributing it.

The decision is not whether there will be cost.

It is where that cost will fall.

This reframes the nature of leadership. The leader is not only choosing an outcome.

He is determining the shape of consequence.

At the level of agency, action is taken with the awareness that no decision will fully align with all responsibilities. The leader can act—but not without producing effects that extend beyond intention. Even well-reasoned decisions generate outcomes that cannot be fully controlled or predicted.

Agency is not diminished.

It is burdened.

Each action carries forward not only intention, but impact.

At the level of legacy, these decisions accumulate. They are not isolated moments, but part of an ongoing pattern of leadership under constraint. The leader may revisit them—not only in terms of effectiveness, but in terms of cost: what was gained, what was lost, who was affected, and how.

These questions do not disappear once a decision is made.

They remain.

This is where moral cost becomes visible. Moral cost in public leadership is not simply the presence of difficult outcomes.

It is the recognition that decisions made in good faith, within appropriate structures, still produce consequences that cannot be fully reconciled with the values the leader seeks to uphold.

The issue is not that the leader does not care.

It is that care cannot be fully enacted at scale without compromise.

At the level of experience, this produces a distinct strain. The leader holds awareness of what the decision accomplishes and what it does not. There is clarity about the rationale, and clarity about the limitation.

These do not cancel each other.

They coexist.

At the level of meaning, moral cost intensifies the divergence already present in compromise. The leader understands the necessity of the decision and remains aware of the ways in which it falls short. Meaning becomes layered—not unclear, but divided across perspectives that cannot be fully reconciled.

At the level of obligation, responsibility does not diminish after the decision is made. The leader remains accountable—not only for implementation, but for consequences, both anticipated and unanticipated.

Responsibility continues.

At the level of judgment, retrospective evaluation becomes more complex. The leader may determine that the decision was justified, necessary, even optimal within the constraints that existed.

And still recognize that it carried cost that cannot be dismissed.

The decision can be sound.

And incomplete.

At the level of agency, the leader cannot return to the moment with new information. The conditions of the decision were specific. The knowledge available was limited to that time. The action taken reflects that context.

There is no version of the decision that removes all cost.

The structure does not allow it.

At the level of legacy, moral cost becomes part of the leader's understanding of the role itself. Leadership is not only about making effective decisions.

It is about carrying the consequences of those decisions over time.

Compromise is not an exception within public life.

It is central to it.

It requires the leader to act within conditions where competing goods must be weighed, where responsibility extends in multiple directions, and where outcomes cannot fully align with all that is valued.

The tension is not that the leader lacks clarity.

It is that clarity itself reveals limitation.

And within that limitation, every decision carries both justification and cost.

PART 3—LEADERSHIP UNDER COMPETING OBLIGATIONS

The decision did not emerge from a single meeting.

It developed over time.

The initial briefing provided structure—data, projections, policy options—but the situation did not remain contained within that frame. As the days progressed, additional information surfaced—not enough to alter the fundamental parameters, but enough to deepen the implications. He continued to review the material, not for clarity, but for consequence.

The issue remained the same, but its effects became more visible. What had been presented as categories and projections took on shape—specific communities, identifiable groups, patterns of impact that extended unevenly across the population. The numbers held, but they did not hold evenly.

At the level of meaning, the situation shifted. The decision was no longer only about selecting a policy option. It became a question of distribution—how impact would be carried, where burden would fall, and who would absorb the consequences of a decision that could not fully satisfy all concerns. He could see this clearly, even as the discussion remained structured around policy.

At the level of obligation, the tension intensified. He was responsible to the system—to act in ways that maintained stability, followed established procedures, and enabled implementation across a broad context. He was also responsible to those affected—to recognize that the effects of the decision would not be evenly experienced. Neither obligation diminished. Both became more specific.

And they did not lead to the same outcome.

He engaged others—colleagues, advisors, individuals who brought different perspectives. The conversations did not produce a single direction.

They clarified the stakes.

Each perspective illuminated a different dimension of the decision. Some emphasized efficiency and feasibility. Others emphasized equity and impact. Some focused on immediate outcomes. Others on long-term consequences. All were valid.

None resolved the tension.

At the level of judgment, the decision began to take form—not as resolution, but as commitment to a particular distribution of consequence. He could not eliminate cost. He could only determine where it would be carried.

He returned to the options—not to identify the best in abstract terms, but to understand how each would shape lived experience. What would this mean for those most affected? What would be gained? What would be lost?

The answers were not symmetrical.

They could not be.

This is where compromise moved from concept to reality. The decision would hold some goods more fully than others, mitigate certain harms while allowing others to remain, and be justified within the system while experienced unevenly outside it.

At the level of agency, he acted—not quickly, but definitively. He chose a path that could be implemented within the system, addressed the most immediate concerns, and aligned with available structures, while knowing it would not fully account for all those affected.

The action did not resolve the tension.

It distributed it.

Part remained within the policy—its limitations, assumptions, and boundaries. Part moved into the lives of those affected, where consequences would be experienced directly. Part stayed with him.

The response unfolded—communication, implementation, public explanation. The decision was articulated in terms that were clear, justified, and grounded in data and responsibility. From the outside, the process reflected effective leadership.

From within, it remained more complex.

At the level of experience, he remained aware of what had not been resolved. The decision functioned as intended within the system, produced measurable outcomes, and addressed the primary concerns identified in the briefing.

And still, it did not fully account for all that he knew.

At the level of outcome, the effects became visible. Some experienced the decision as necessary, even beneficial. Others experienced it as insufficient, burdensome, or harmful. Both interpretations were accurate—from their respective positions.

At the level of retrospective meaning, he revisited the decision—not to question whether it had been required, but to consider how it had held the competing obligations present in the moment. He could see the structure clearly—the data, the options, the consultations, the choice. The reasoning held. The necessity remained.

And yet, something did not fully resolve.

He had acted within responsibility to the system.

He had considered those affected.

And still, he could not say that both had been fully satisfied.

At the level of retrospective obligation, the tension persisted. Responsibility did not end with the decision. It continued in its consequences—anticipated and unanticipated. The leader remained accountable not only for what had been chosen, but for how it unfolded.

The obligations had been engaged.

Not reconciled.

At the level of retrospective judgment, he evaluated the decision again. He could justify it within the constraints that existed, explain why this path had been chosen, and demonstrate that it was reasonable, necessary, and aligned with available information.

The decision was sound.

But it was not complete.

At the level of retrospective agency, there was no alternative that removed the cost. A different decision would have shifted the burden, not eliminated it. To act differently would have changed who was affected, not whether someone would be.

There was no version of the moment without consequence.

The structure does not allow it.

At the level of legacy, the experience did not remain isolated. It became part of his understanding of leadership—not as the selection of optimal solutions, but as the navigation of competing obligations under constraint. He recognized that this was not an exception.

It was the work.

The pattern became clearer. Decisions at this level will continue to require compromise, produce uneven outcomes, and carry moral cost that cannot be fully resolved. He was not only remembering the decision.

He was recognizing the nature of the role.

This is where public leadership reveals its deeper demand. It is not only the application of policy and not only the management of outcomes.

It is the acceptance of consequence.

The leader is not only choosing between options.

He is determining how cost is carried.

The policy did not fail.

The people did not disappear.

The system did not collapse.

The tension remained.

And in that tension, the decision carried weight.

Not because it was wrong.

But because it could not be complete.

PART 4—DECISION-MAKING UNDER MORAL PRESSURE: MIR + M.O.R.A.L IN PRACTICE

When policy and people do not fully align, the instinct is to force clarity—to treat one dimension as primary and the other as secondary. The pressure to simplify is strong. Systems require decisiveness. People require responsiveness.

But public leadership resists that simplification.

The task is not to eliminate the tension.

It is to act within it with clarity and integrity.

What is not processed in the moment does not disappear.

It accumulates.

The first movement is recognition. Recognition names the condition accurately. The leader is not failing to decide, and the leader is not failing to care. The leader is operating within a context where competing goods cannot be fully reconciled. This distinction is essential: it is not that I chose wrong; it is that full alignment was not available. Recognition interrupts the tendency to interpret tension as failure and locates the experience within the nature of public leadership itself, allowing the leader to remain engaged without misidentifying the work.

The second movement is differentiating between policy function and human impact. Policy organizes complexity, enables coordinated action, and creates consistency at scale. Human impact is experienced in particular—unevenly, directly, and often outside the abstractions that policy requires. Both are real. Both are necessary. But they are not the same. The leader must hold both—not as competing errors, but as competing goods.

The tension is not between system and care.

It is between function and experience.

The third movement is applying MIR under moral pressure. MIR—Minimize, Interpret, Re-engage—stabilizes decision-making without collapsing complexity. Minimize reduces distortion by identifying what is essential in the moment—what must be preserved within the system, what must be considered in terms of impact, and what cannot be fully resolved within the current decision. This clarifies the field without denying its limits. Interpret makes meaning within constraint. The leader does not wait for complete alignment between policy and people, but works with the alignment that is available, drawing on experience, ethical reasoning, and contextual awareness to determine a course of action that holds integrity across competing demands. Re-engage continues the work without requiring that the tension be resolved, carrying awareness forward without allowing it to halt action.

MIR does not remove moral pressure.

It stabilizes action within it.

The fourth movement is engaging the M.O.R.A.L framework within public leadership. At the level of meaning, the leader recognizes that decisions are interpreted differently across contexts—within the system and among those affected—preventing reduction to a single narrative. At the level of obligation, the leader acknowledges multiple responsibilities—to institutional continuity, to public trust, and to the lived experiences of those impacted. These obligations are simultaneous and cannot always be reconciled. At the level of judgment, the leader evaluates based on integrity rather than resolution; the question is not whether the decision satisfies all demands, but whether it holds the most responsible balance within existing constraints. At the level of agency, the leader acts within limitation—aware that every decision distributes consequence. Action is taken not because it removes cost, but because it responds responsibly.

Agency is not simplified.

It is burdened.

At the level of legacy, the leader anticipates that these decisions will remain. They are not erased by justification or outcome. They become part of the ongoing experience of leadership, shaping future decisions and the understanding of the role itself.

The fifth movement is resisting retrospective distortion. After the decision, there is a tendency to impose simplified narratives—to treat the outcome as either fully justified or fundamentally flawed without returning to the conditions as they were. Resisting distortion requires returning to the moment of decision—what was known, what constraints were present, what options were available. The question is not what would have been ideal.

It is what could be done.

This prevents hindsight from collapsing complexity into false clarity.

The sixth movement is re-engaging these decisions in community. Public leadership is not solitary, even when decisions are carried by individuals. Processing these moments with trusted colleagues, advisors, and stakeholders allows for shared reflection. The goal is not consensus.

It is shared accountability.

The weight is not removed.

It is distributed.

The seventh movement is integrating policy and people without collapsing either. The leader learns to hold system function and human impact without allowing one to erase the other. Policy remains. People remain.

Integration does not resolve the gap.

It makes it governable.

Working in public leadership is not about achieving perfect alignment between policy and people. It is about sustaining responsible action within their divergence—moving from assumed failure to recognized structure, from forced clarity to held complexity, from isolated decision to shared accountability, from accumulation to integration.

The system does not disappear.

The people do not disappear.

The gap remains.

But the leader learns to stand within it.

And decide.

REFLECTION

When you make decisions that affect others, how do you understand your role?

As decision-maker?

As steward?

As something more?

When policy and people do not fully align, what do you experience first?

Clarity?

Pressure?

Weight?

How do you interpret that experience?

As failure?

As responsibility?

As part of the role?

What do you feel most accountable to in those moments?

The system?

The outcome?

The people affected?

How do those priorities shape what you decide?

When you know a decision will carry uneven impact, how do you hold that?

Do you try to minimize it?

Justify it?

Distribute it?

What does "fair" mean to you in that context?

When you think about compromise, what do you believe it represents?

Weakness?

Necessity?

Wisdom?

What changes when you understand compromise as a function of scale rather than a loss of conviction?

When you look back on your decisions, what do you notice?

Do you see clarity that was not available at the time?

Do you measure yourself by that clarity?

What shifts when you return to the conditions as they were?

What was known?

What constraints were present?

What could be done?

Where do you carry the cost of your decisions?

Internally?

Relationally?

Structurally?

How do you process that cost?

Alone?

With others?

Within systems that recognize it?

What difference does that make?

What patterns do you begin to see in how you decide?

What do those patterns reveal about how you understand responsibility?

How do you hold the tension between what a decision accomplishes and what it leaves unresolved?

Do you try to close that gap?

Or learn to live within it?

What would it mean to lead without requiring that policy and people always fully align?

What would it require to act within that tension—without turning away from either?

WHAT'S NEXT

We have seen how moral injury emerges in roles of authority and responsibility.

Next, we will turn toward response—how moral injury is recognized in real time.

SECTION IV

Response and Repair

Chapter 14

Recognizing Moral Injury

PART 1—THE MOMENT OF REALIZATION

IT DID NOT ARRIVE at the moment of decision.

It came later.

At first, everything appeared to move forward as expected. The decision had been made. The process had unfolded. The responsibilities had been carried. From the outside, the work continued without interruption. The system remained intact. The role remained clear. There was no immediate disruption, no visible break.

But something had shifted—not in the structure, but in him.

It was not a single thought or feeling, but a change in orientation—subtle at first, difficult to name, easy to dismiss. The work continued, but the experience of the work was no longer the same. He noticed it in moments that would once have passed without attention—a hesitation where there had been ease, a weight where there had been clarity, a question that did not resolve even after the decision had been justified.

Nothing had gone wrong.

And still, something was not as it had been.

At first, he interpreted it as fatigue. The demands of the role had been significant. The decisions had required sustained attention. It made sense that there would be a period of adjustment. He continued.

But the experience did not recede.

It remained.

It began to appear in different forms—discomfort in conversations that once felt familiar, reluctance to engage certain situations, a heightened awareness of decisions that carried similar patterns. It was not constant, but it was persistent.

At the level of experience, this is how moral injury often begins—not as rupture, but as recognition that something has been carried that does not easily settle. There is no clear boundary, no single moment of identification—only the growing awareness that the work has left something behind.

He began to revisit the decision—not because it required correction, but because it continued to surface. He could explain it. He could justify it. He could align it with responsibility and structure.

And still, it remained present.

This is where the shift deepens. The issue is no longer the decision itself.

It is the relationship to it.

At the level of meaning, interpretation begins to change. What was once understood as necessary and appropriate remains so, but is now accompanied by the awareness that necessity does not remove impact.

The decision was sound.

And it carried cost.

These realities do not cancel each other.

They coexist.

At the level of obligation, responsibility extends beyond action. The leader begins to sense that responsibility is not only about making the decision, but about carrying what follows from it. This is not assigned.

It is experienced.

He did not choose to carry it.

And yet, he did.

At the level of judgment, evaluation becomes layered. The question is no longer only whether the decision was right within the conditions that existed.

It becomes:

What does it mean that this decision continues to remain with me?

This is not a question of error.

It is a question of impact.

At the level of agency, there is a subtle shift. The leader continues to act, decide, and engage in the work, but now action is accompanied by awareness—not avoidance, not withdrawal, but recognition. Something has been added to the experience of acting, and it cannot be set aside.

At the level of legacy, the moment takes on a different quality. It is no longer only part of the sequence of decisions that define the role.

It becomes part of how the role is experienced.

The decision is no longer only something that was made.

It is something that is carried.

This is where moral injury becomes visible—not as a dramatic rupture, but as sustained awareness that certain experiences do not fully resolve within the structures that required them. The system accounted for the decision.

It did not account for what remained.

He did not arrive at this realization all at once. It emerged gradually—through repetition, reflection, and the accumulation of moments that did not fully return to equilibrium. He began to notice patterns—similar situations producing similar weight, different contexts carrying the same residue.

The details changed.

The experience did not.

This is where recognition takes form—not as diagnosis, but as acknowledgment. Something is happening here—something not explained by fatigue alone, not resolved by justification, something that persists even when the work has been done as it should have been.

He did not yet name it.

But he no longer dismissed it.

This is the moment of realization—not a break, not a failure, but recognition.

The work has left something behind.

And it remains.

PART 2—INDICATORS, PATTERNS, AND LANGUAGE

The experience described in the previous section does not immediately present itself as moral injury.

It rarely names itself.

More often, it appears as a series of indicators—subtle at first, then recurring, then increasingly difficult to dismiss. These indicators do not point to a single event, but to a pattern. They do not announce a condition.

They accumulate into one.

This is what makes recognition difficult. The leader does not encounter moral injury as a clear diagnosis, but as a disruption in continuity—an experience that does not return to baseline, even when the work has been carried out as required.

At the level of experience, the first indicators appear as shifts in engagement. Situations that once felt familiar begin to carry weight. Decisions once approached with clarity now include hesitation. The leader may not withdraw from the work, but the experience of the work changes—it becomes heavier, more deliberate, less easily resolved. These shifts are not constant, but they are persistent, reappearing across contexts, decisions, and time.

This persistence is the first pattern—not intensity, but recurrence.

At the level of meaning, interpretation begins to fragment. The leader continues to understand the rationale behind decisions—why they were made, how they align with responsibility, how they function within the system. That understanding does not disappear.

But it is no longer sufficient.

A second layer emerges—an awareness that justification does not fully account for impact. The leader holds two interpretations at once: the decision as necessary, and the decision as carrying something unresolved. These interpretations do not cancel each other.

They remain.

This fragmentation is the second pattern—not confusion, but division.

At the level of obligation, responsibility extends beyond action. The leader begins to feel accountable not only for the decision, but for its consequences in a way not fully defined by role or structure. Responsibility continues even when formal responsibility has been fulfilled. This is not always articulated.

It is experienced.

The leader returns to situations, reconsiders outcomes, and carries an ongoing connection to what has occurred.

This extension is the third pattern—not assignment, but continuation.

At the level of judgment, evaluation becomes layered. The leader can assess the decision as appropriate within the conditions that existed, recognize that it was necessary, justified, even effective—

And still experience that something within it does not settle.

The question shifts—not from "Was this right?" but from "Why does this remain?"

This persistence of evaluation is the fourth pattern—not doubt, but endurance.

At the level of agency, action continues, but with altered awareness. The leader does not disengage from the role, but each action carries an added dimension—an awareness of what decisions leave behind. This does not prevent action.

But it changes it.

Action becomes more deliberate, more weighted, more conscious of consequence.

This alteration is the fifth pattern—not paralysis, but awareness.

At the level of legacy, these experiences accumulate. The leader may not identify each moment individually, but over time, a pattern emerges. Certain decisions and situations produce a similar internal response. The details vary.

The residue does not.

This accumulation is the sixth pattern—not isolated events, but continuity.

Taken together, these patterns form a structure of recognition. Moral injury is not identified through a single indicator, but through the convergence of experience over time. It is not the presence of weight.

It is the persistence of it.

It is not the existence of difficult decisions.

It is the way those decisions remain.

This is where language becomes necessary. Without language, the experience remains diffuse—felt, but not defined. The leader may sense that something is present, but without a way to name it, the experience is often misattributed to fatigue, stress, or the ordinary demands of the role.

These explanations are not incorrect.

But they are incomplete.

Language does not create the experience.

It clarifies it.

To name moral injury is not to pathologize the leader.

It is to recognize a condition that emerges when responsibility, action, and consequence do not fully reconcile. The language must be precise—not exaggerated, not diminished—and able to hold complexity without reduction.

Moral injury is not simply emotional distress. It is not only ethical conflict. It is not reducible to burnout.

It is the sustained impact of acting within conditions where what is required cannot fully align with what is valued—and where that misalignment remains.

This definition does not resolve the experience.

It makes it visible.

Recognition, then, is not the elimination of uncertainty.

It is the clarification of what is being experienced.

The leader does not move from confusion to certainty.

He moves from unarticulated experience to named condition.

This is the threshold.

Not the end of the process.

But it's beginning.

INTERLUDE—WHEN RECOGNITION IS DELAYED

Recognition does not always arrive when the experience begins.

Often, it is deferred.

The indicators are present. The patterns are forming. The experience has already begun to shift, but the leader does not interpret these signals as significant. They are absorbed into the existing understanding of the role—explained as part of the work, part of the demand, part of what is required. Nothing appears out of place, because everything appears familiar.

This is one of the defining characteristics of moral injury—it emerges within contexts already understood as difficult. The leader is accustomed to weight, complexity, and decisions that carry consequence. Difficulty is not new. Tension is not new. Responsibility is not new.

So when something changes, it is not recognized as change.

It is interpreted as more of the same.

At the level of experience, this produces a kind of normalization. The hesitation, the weight, the persistence of certain thoughts—these are not identified as indicators. They are folded into the rhythm of the work and become part of what is expected.

This is just how it is.

This is what it requires.

This is what the role asks.

And in that interpretation, recognition is delayed.

At the level of meaning, the delay is reinforced by competence. The leader continues to function. Decisions are made. Responsibilities are carried. From the outside, there is no disruption. The work continues to be done well. This creates a powerful reinforcement:

If I am still able to do the work, then nothing is wrong.

But moral injury does not interrupt function.

It alters experience.

And those two are not the same.

At the level of obligation, the delay deepens. The leader feels an increasing responsibility not only to act, but to continue acting without interruption. To pause, question, or examine the internal experience feels like a failure to meet the demands of the role. So the work continues, and the experience is carried forward with it—unexamined, unnamed, but not absent.

At the level of judgment, this produces a subtle distortion. Because the decision can be justified, because the action aligns with responsibility, and because the outcome can be explained, the internal persistence is interpreted as unnecessary—something that should resolve, pass, or not remain. When it does remain, the question turns inward:

Why is this still with me?

Why has this not settled?

This question is not yet recognition.

It is misrecognition.

It assumes that what persists should not persist and frames the experience as something to be corrected rather than understood.

At the level of agency, the leader continues to act, but with a growing distance between action and experience. The work is still carried out effectively. The decisions are still made. The role is still fulfilled.

But the internal alignment continues to shift.

Not enough to stop the work.

But enough to change it.

This is where delayed recognition becomes decisive. The longer the experience remains unnamed, the more it accumulates without structure. Patterns form but are not identified. Indicators repeat but are not interpreted. The leader adapts, but without clarity.

At the level of legacy, this accumulation begins to shape the experience of the role itself. What was once carried as isolated moments takes on continuity—not because each moment is overwhelming, but because none have been fully processed. The weight is not singular.

It is layered.

Because it has not been named, it does not yet have a place within the leader's understanding of the work. It exists without orientation, is carried without context, and is felt without language.

This is why recognition matters—not because it changes what has happened, but because it changes how what has happened is held. To recognize moral injury is not to introduce something new, but to see what has already been present—to move from carrying without clarity

to carrying with awareness.

This shift is not dramatic.

But it is decisive.

It does not resolve the experience.

It reorients it.

The leader is no longer asking only how to continue.

He begins to ask what he is carrying as he does.

And in that question, recognition takes hold—not as conclusion, but as clarity.

Not as resolution.

But as understanding.

PART 3—IDENTIFYING MORAL INJURY IN REAL TIME

The recognition did not happen in reflection alone.

It began in the moment.

He was in a conversation that, on the surface, did not differ significantly from others he had navigated before. The structure was familiar. The expectations were clear. The role remained intact. Nothing in the situation suggested that this moment would be different.

And yet, it was.

He noticed it first as hesitation—not a pause for clarity, but a pause that did not resolve. The information was sufficient. The options were understood. The decision pathway was recognizable.

But something did not move.

He continued. He engaged. He responded as required. From the outside, nothing had changed, but internally the experience did not align with the action.

At the level of experience, recognition begins not after the fact, but within the act itself. The leader senses a disruption in continuity. The work proceeds, but it does not feel the same.

The action is carried.

The alignment is not.

He became aware of a familiar pattern—not in the details of the situation, but in the response it produced. The weight was recognizable. The sense of carrying something forward was already present, even before the decision had been completed.

This was not new.

It had happened before.

At the level of meaning, interpretation began to divide in real time. He understood the situation within the framework of responsibility—what was required, what could be justified, what aligned with the role—while also recognizing that this understanding did not fully account for what was happening within him.

Both interpretations were present.

Simultaneously.

Neither displaced the other.

At the level of obligation, the tension emerged before the decision was finalized. He felt responsible to act—to carry out the requirements of the role, to engage the situation as it demanded—while also sensing that what would follow would not end with the action itself.

The obligation did not begin after the decision.

It was already present within it.

At the level of judgment, evaluation began before completion. He was not waiting to assess the outcome; he was already aware that this moment would remain. The question was not only what should be done.

It was what this would become once it was done.

This awareness did not prevent action.

But it altered it.

At the level of agency, he continued. He spoke. He acted. He moved the situation forward within the structures available to him. From the outside, the decision unfolded as expected; from within, it was accompanied by recognition.

This would not end here.

The action was not interrupted.

But it was not unmarked.

At the level of legacy, the moment registered immediately. It did not need time to settle or distance to be understood as significant. It was already known—not in full clarity, but in form.

This was something that would remain.

This is the distinction between reflection and recognition. Reflection occurs after the moment, when distance allows for evaluation. Recognition occurs within the moment, when the experience itself signals that something is being carried.

He did not stop the process, withdraw, or alter the decision in a way that would disrupt the system.

But he no longer moved through the moment without awareness.

This awareness changed the nature of the work. The decision was still made. The process still unfolded. The role was still fulfilled.

And yet, something additional was present.

He recognized the pattern—not abstractly or theoretically, but in real time. The indicators described earlier—persistence, division, continuation, endurance, awareness, accumulation—were no longer concepts.

They were occurring.

Within the act.

This is where identification becomes possible. Moral injury is not only recognized after the fact. It can be identified as it is forming—through the awareness that the experience is already taking shape in ways that will not easily resolve.

This recognition does not stop the work or remove the necessity of action.

But it changes the relationship to it.

The leader is no longer moving through the moment without context.

He is aware of what the moment is becoming.

At the level of experience, this awareness is not overwhelming.

It is clarifying.

At the level of meaning, it does not simplify.

It deepens.

At the level of obligation, it does not reduce responsibility.

It expands it.

At the level of judgment, it does not resolve the decision.

It situates it.

At the level of agency, it does not prevent action.

It accompanies it.

At the level of legacy, it does not wait.

It begins.

He did not name it immediately.

But he recognized it.

And in that recognition, something shifted—not in what he did, but in how he understood what he was doing.

This is the moment where moral injury becomes identifiable—not as something that has already occurred, but as something actively forming within the work itself.

It is not a conclusion.

It is an awareness.

And once seen, it cannot be unseen.

PART 4—FULL ASSESSMENT: MIR + M.O.R.A.L IN PRACTICE

Recognition alone is not sufficient.

To recognize that something is present is the beginning.

To understand it, name it, and work with it requires structure.

Without structure, the experience remains diffuse—felt, but not clarified. It may be acknowledged, but not engaged. It may be carried, but not examined.

This is where assessment becomes necessary—not as diagnosis, but as orientation. The purpose of assessment is not to reduce moral injury to a checklist, but to create a way of seeing that allows the leader to identify what is happening without collapsing its complexity.

The first movement is returning to MIR—Minimize, Interpret, Re-engage—not as steps to complete, but as movements to inhabit.

Minimize reduces distortion. In the context of moral injury, distortion often appears as misattribution—interpreting the experience as fatigue, personal failure, or isolated stress. These interpretations are not entirely incorrect.

But they are incomplete.

To minimize is to ask what is actually present—not what is easiest to name, but what persists beneath explanation. This requires attention to pattern—what repeats, what endures, what does not return to baseline.

Minimize does not remove the experience.

It clarifies it.

Interpret makes meaning without forcing resolution. Once the experience is clarified, the question becomes what it represents—not in abstraction, but in lived connection. Which decisions, responsibilities, and moments of tension continue to remain?

Interpretation does not collapse the experience into a single conclusion.

It allows multiple layers to coexist—the decision as necessary, the decision as costly, the decision as unresolved.

Interpret does not resolve tension.

It names it.

Re-engage returns the leader to the work with awareness. Recognition and interpretation do not remove responsibility. The role continues. Decisions continue.

Re-engagement is not a return to unawareness.

It is a continuation with clarity.

The leader does not wait for the experience to resolve before acting.

He carries it.

With understanding.

MIR stabilizes the process.

It does not complete it.

The second movement is applying the full M.O.R.A.L framework as an assessment lens.

At the level of meaning, the leader asks how the experience is being interpreted. Is there a division between what is understood as necessary and what remains unresolved? Are multiple interpretations being held at once?

Meaning is not assessed by clarity alone.

It is assessed by layering.

At the level of obligation, the leader asks what responsibilities are present, which have been fulfilled, and which continue to feel active. Is there a sense that responsibility extends beyond the action itself?

Obligation is not limited to role.

It is experienced as continuation.

At the level of judgment, the leader asks how the decision is being evaluated. Is the evaluation stable, or does it return? Is the question about correctness, or about persistence?

Judgment is not only about whether something was right.

It is about why it remains.

At the level of agency, the leader asks how the experience has altered action. Is there increased hesitation, deliberation, or awareness? Is action continuing, but differently?

Agency is not assessed by whether action occurs.

It is assessed by how it is experienced.

At the level of legacy, the leader asks whether the moment is isolated or connected. Are patterns emerging? Is this becoming part of how the role is understood?

Legacy is not only what is remembered.

It is what accumulates.

Taken together, these questions form a field of assessment. The leader does not move through them once, but repeatedly, as the experience unfolds.

Assessment is not a single act.

It is an ongoing orientation.

The third movement is recognizing thresholds. Not every difficult decision results in moral injury. Not every experience of strain carries lasting impact.

The distinction is not intensity.

It is persistence.

When the experience does not resolve—when it remains across time, explanation, and context, when it begins to form patterns—this marks a threshold.

Not of certainty.

Of recognition.

The fourth movement is resisting premature resolution. Once moral injury is recognized, there is often a desire to resolve it—to restore alignment, find closure, and reach a clear conclusion.

This impulse is understandable.

But it can distort the process.

Moral injury is not resolved through immediate explanation. It requires time, reflection, and often shared engagement.

The task is not to close the experience.

It is to understand it.

The fifth movement is situating the experience within the role. Moral injury does not occur outside the work.

It emerges from it.

To recognize moral injury is not to step away from leadership, but to understand what leadership requires and what it leaves behind. This reframes the experience—not as interruption, but as condition.

The sixth movement is preparing for continuation. Recognition does not end the work.

It changes it.

The leader continues to act, now with awareness of what the work carries. This awareness does not eliminate future moral strain, but it changes how it is encountered—with language, structure, and recognition.

The final movement is integration—not as resolution, but as incorporation. The experience is not removed from the leader's understanding of the role.

It becomes part of it.

Not as something that defines the leader.

But as something that informs him.

Integration does not eliminate the weight.

It allows it to be carried with clarity.

REFLECTION

When you begin to sense that something remains, how do you respond?

Do you explain it?

Dismiss it?

Carry it without naming it?

What changes when you ask what is actually present—not what is easiest to say, but what continues?

When you revisit a decision, what draws your attention?

The outcome?

The reasoning?

Or the fact that it still remains?

How do you interpret that persistence?

As error?

As responsibility?

As something else?

Where do you feel responsibility continuing beyond action?

How do you understand that?

When you evaluate your decisions, do your questions resolve—or return?

How has your experience of acting changed?

More hesitant?

More deliberate?

More aware?

What patterns are beginning to emerge?

Do they connect?

Do they accumulate?

At what point does difficulty become something more—not because it is intense, but because it remains?

What would it mean to recognize that without needing to resolve it immediately?

WHAT'S NEXT

We now have tools to recognize moral injury as it is present.

Next, we will move into care and conversation—how to remain with others in what does not resolve.

Chapter 15

Care and Conversation

PART 1—SITTING WITH SOMEONE IN MORAL PAIN

He did not come asking for help.

He came to talk.

There was no formal request, no clear framing of the conversation as something to be addressed. It began the way many of these conversations begin—indirectly, without declaration, without structure. He mentioned a situation—not in detail, not all at once, just enough to begin.

The context was familiar. A decision had been made. The conditions had been difficult. The outcome had been carried. Nothing in what he said suggested failure. Nothing indicated that something had gone wrong.

And yet, he had returned to it.

More than once.

At first, it sounded like reflection—the kind that often follows significant responsibility. He described what had happened, how the decision had been made, what factors had been considered. He spoke with clarity, coherence, and justification.

But the conversation did not move forward.

It circled.

He returned to the same moment, the same detail, the same point of decision—not to explain it, but because it had not settled.

The listener did not interrupt, redirect, or attempt to resolve.

He stayed.

This is where care begins—not in intervention, but in presence. The instinct to help often moves toward action: to clarify, reassure, offer perspective, or guide the conversation toward resolution.

But this was not a situation that required fixing.

It required space.

The speaker continued. The story did not unfold in sequence. It moved in fragments—returning, revisiting, pausing, beginning again. What mattered was not the order of events.

It was the persistence of them.

The listener noticed what was repeating—not only in content, but in tone. Certain parts of the story carried more weight. Certain phrases returned. Certain moments were approached, then left, then approached again.

This is where attention shifts—not to what is being said, but to what is remaining.

At the level of experience, the speaker was not simply recounting an event. He was expressing something that had not resolved within it. The details of the decision were intact. The reasoning was clear.

But the experience continued.

At the level of meaning, both interpretations were present. The decision had been necessary. It had been justified. It had aligned with responsibility.

And it had carried something that remained.

The speaker did not state this directly.

But it was present in the way he returned.

At the level of obligation, the sense of responsibility had not ended with the decision. It extended into the present—not as formal accountability, but as something still being carried. The speaker was not only describing what had happened.

He was holding it.

At the level of judgment, there was no explicit questioning of whether the decision had been right. That question had already been addressed. What remained was something else—not doubt, but persistence.

The listener did not name it.

He allowed it to be present.

At the level of agency, the speaker continued to engage—not withdrawing, not avoiding, but also not resolving. The conversation itself became part of the process—not as a means to an answer, but as a way of holding what had not settled.

The listener did not take control of the conversation.

He did not move it toward conclusion.

He stayed with it.

At the level of legacy, the moment revealed itself—not as a single event, but as something already beginning to accumulate. This was not the first time the speaker had returned to this experience.

And it would not be the last.

This is where care takes shape—not as intervention, but as accompaniment. The listener's role was not to fix the experience, reinterpret the decision, or resolve the tension. It was to remain present to what was being carried—without reducing it, redirecting it, or attempting to make it something other than it was.

Presence is not passive.

It is disciplined.

It requires restraint—the ability to remain without filling the space, to listen without moving ahead, to recognize without naming prematurely.

The listener noticed the impulse to help—to offer reassurance, provide explanation, or suggest that the decision had been necessary and therefore should not continue to carry weight.

All of these would have been true.

And all of them would have missed the moment.

Because the issue was not whether the decision had been justified.

It was that it remained.

To move too quickly toward resolution would have shifted the conversation away from what was present and back toward what had already been addressed.

So the listener stayed.

He allowed silence when it came. He followed when the speaker returned to the same place. He did not interpret repetition as lack of clarity.

He understood it as indication.

Something here has not settled.

And it is being carried.

Over time, the conversation deepened—not because new information was introduced, but because what had been present was allowed to remain in view. The speaker began to speak more directly—not about the decision itself, but about the experience of carrying it.

Not as explanation.

But as acknowledgment.

The listener did not change the content of the conversation.

He changed the conditions in which it could occur.

This is the work of care in the presence of moral injury—not to resolve what cannot be resolved, remove what remains, or correct what is not an error, but to create a space in which the experience can be held without distortion, urgency, or reduction.

The conversation did not end with resolution.

It ended with recognition.

Not because something had been fixed.

But because something had been allowed to be seen.

PART 2—PRESENCE OVER FIXING

The instinct to help is immediate.

It arises as soon as another person begins to speak about something that carries weight. The listener hears tension, repetition, what does not resolve—and moves, almost automatically, toward response: to clarify, reassure, interpret, resolve.

This instinct is not misplaced.

It is trained.

In most domains, difficulty is approached as something to be addressed. Problems are identified, analyzed, and solved. Uncertainty is reduced through explanation. Distress is met with intervention. These patterns are effective.

They are necessary.

But they do not apply in the same way to moral injury.

Moral injury is not a problem to be solved.

It is an experience to be carried.

When the listener approaches it as something to fix, the conversation begins to move away from what is present.

At the level of experience, fixing introduces distance. The speaker is describing something that remains—something that has not settled, something that continues to carry weight. When the listener responds with explanation or reassurance, the focus shifts from the persistence of the experience to the logic of the decision.

The conversation moves from:

This remains.

To:

This makes sense.

Both may be true.

But they are not the same.

At the level of meaning, fixing reduces complexity. It selects one interpretation—often the most stable, justifiable, and coherent—and reinforces it. The decision was necessary. The conditions were difficult. The outcome was unavoidable.

These statements may be accurate.

But they do not hold the full experience.

They do not account for what continues.

Presence, by contrast, allows multiple meanings to coexist. It does not force resolution between them or require the experience to align into a single interpretation.

It holds:

This was necessary.

And this remains.

At the level of obligation, fixing narrows responsibility. It returns the conversation to what was required at the time of decision—what had to be done, what could not be avoided, what was justified.

Presence expands responsibility—not by assigning additional burden, but by acknowledging that responsibility does not always end with action. It recognizes that what follows from a decision may continue to be carried, even when the decision itself was appropriate.

Fixing resolves responsibility.

Presence recognizes its continuation.

At the level of judgment, fixing seeks closure. It answers whether the decision was right, whether the action was justified, whether the outcome was acceptable.

Presence shifts the question.

Not:

Was this right?

But:

What remains from this?

This shift is subtle.

But decisive.

It moves the conversation from evaluation to recognition.

At the level of agency, fixing directs. It introduces guidance, suggests alternative perspectives, and moves the speaker toward a different understanding.

Presence accompanies.

It does not remove the speaker's agency.

It remains alongside it.

It allows the speaker to continue moving through the experience without being redirected away from it.

This does not mean the listener is passive.

It means the listener is disciplined.

At the level of legacy, fixing isolates the moment. It treats the experience as something that can be resolved within the conversation—as something that can be addressed and concluded.

Presence situates the moment within a larger pattern. It recognizes that this is not only about what happened, but about how what happened continues to exist within the person speaking.

It understands that the conversation is not the endpoint.

It is part of an ongoing process.

This is why presence is more difficult than fixing. Fixing offers movement. Presence requires stillness. Fixing provides answers. Presence allows questions to remain. Fixing brings the conversation to a point.

Presence keeps it open.

This does not mean fixing is always inappropriate. There are situations that require intervention, clarification, and direction. There are moments where action is necessary, where misunderstanding must be corrected, where decisions must be guided.

But in the presence of moral injury, the primary need is not correction.

It is recognition.

The listener must learn to distinguish between these conditions—to recognize when the instinct to fix is appropriate and when it is a way of moving away from what is difficult to hold.

This requires attention—not only to what is being said, but to what is happening within the listener. The impulse to fix is often a response to discomfort: the weight of what is being heard, the absence of resolution, the recognition that there is no clear way to make this easier.

In that moment, fixing becomes a form of relief.

For the listener.

Not for the speaker.

Presence requires the listener to remain within that discomfort without attempting to remove it. It requires the ability to hear what does not resolve without forcing it into resolution.

This is not passive.

It is active restraint.

The listener listens for what repeats—for what returns, for what carries weight. He allows silence. He follows the speaker's movement. He resists the urge to complete what has not been completed.

Over time, this changes the conversation—not by introducing new content, but by allowing what is already present to be more fully expressed. The speaker does not need to defend the decision, justify the experience, or resolve what cannot be resolved.

The conversation becomes a place where both can be held.

This is what presence makes possible.

Not resolution.

But recognition.

PART 3—CARE INTERACTION WALKTHROUGH

The conversation does not begin with structure.

It begins with attention.

The speaker returns to the moment—not all at once, not in sequence, but in fragments. A detail is offered, then another, then a pause. The listener does not organize the narrative or move it toward clarity.

He follows.

This is the first movement—staying with what is given.

At the level of experience, the listener attends not only to what is said, but to how it is said. Where does the speaker hesitate? Where does the voice shift? What returns more than once? The content matters, but the pattern matters more.

The speaker describes the decision. The conditions were constrained. The options were limited. The outcome was necessary. The listener does not interrupt. He allows the description to stand, but notices where the speaker returns—a phrase repeated, a moment revisited, a detail approached, then left, then approached again.

This is where the second movement begins—recognizing without naming. The listener does not identify the pattern explicitly or call attention to it.

He allows it to continue.

At the level of meaning, the speaker holds two interpretations—one articulated, one implied. The articulated meaning is clear: the decision was justified. The implied meaning is less direct: something within it remains. The listener does not resolve this or choose one interpretation over the other.

He holds both.

He reflects what is present without collapsing it:

"You're clear about why the decision had to be made."

And then, after a pause:

"And it still seems to stay with you."

This is not interpretation.

It is recognition.

The speaker pauses—not because something new has been introduced, but because something already present has been named without reduction.

At the level of obligation, the speaker reveals continuation. The decision is in the past, but the sense of responsibility is not. It extends into the present—not as formal accountability, but as something still being carried.

"I know it was the right call."

Pause.

"But I still think about it."

The listener does not reassure or return to justification.

He stays with the continuation:

"It hasn't ended for you."

This is the third movement—following responsibility beyond the moment.

At the level of judgment, the speaker does not question the correctness of the decision. That has already been resolved. What remains is something else. The listener does not return to evaluation.

He stays with the persistence:

"It's not about whether it was right."

Pause.

"It's that it's still here."

The speaker nods—not because he has learned something new, but because what he has been experiencing has been recognized.

At the level of agency, the speaker continues. The story does not conclude; it deepens. The listener does not direct the conversation or move it toward resolution.

He allows the speaker to continue moving through the experience.

This is not passive listening.

It is active restraint.

The listener notices the impulse to fix—to offer explanation, provide reassurance, or reduce the weight of the experience.

He does not act on it.

He stays.

At the level of legacy, the pattern becomes clearer. This is not the only moment the speaker has carried. There are others—similar in structure, similar in weight. The listener does not expand the conversation prematurely.

He allows the speaker to make that connection.

Over time, the speaker begins to speak differently—not only about what happened, but about what remains, more directly and with less fragmentation. The conversation shifts—not because the listener introduced something new, but because he did not remove what was already there.

This is the fourth movement—creating conditions for recognition. The listener does not summarize, conclude, or resolve. He reflects selectively—only what carries weight, what returns, what remains. He allows silence, repetition, and openness.

This is where care takes form—not as technique, but as posture.

The conversation does not produce an answer.

It produces clarity.

Not about the decision.

But about the experience.

The speaker is not told what to do, guided toward resolution, or reassured out of what he is carrying.

He is accompanied.

And in that accompaniment, something becomes possible—not the removal of what remains, but the ability to recognize it without distortion.

This is the work—not to fix, resolve, or conclude, but to remain present long enough for what is carried to be seen.

PART 4—CONVERSATION GUIDES AND BOUNDARIES

Care requires more than intention.

It requires form.

Without form, the conversation drifts—toward fixing, avoidance, or over-identification. The listener may remain present in intention, but lose clarity in practice. This is where guidance becomes necessary—not as script, but as orientation. The purpose of these guides is not to control the conversation.

It is to help the listener remain within it.

The first movement is returning to MIR within conversation—Minimize, Interpret, Re-engage—not as an internal process alone, but as relational practice.

Minimize reduces distortion in what is heard and what is said. The listener avoids translating the speaker's experience into something more manageable—avoiding premature reassurance, explanation, or reframing. Instead of saying, "You did what you had to do," the listener remains close to what is present: "It sounds like that hasn't settled."

Minimize does not simplify the experience.

It protects it from reduction.

Interpret involves naming without closing. The listener reflects what is emerging—not as conclusion, but as recognition. The language remains tentative, open, and grounded in what the speaker has already expressed.

"You keep coming back to that moment."

"There's something there that stays with you."

This is not analysis.

It is articulation.

Interpret does not resolve the experience.

It gives it form.

Re-engage means staying with the speaker as the experience unfolds. The listener does not move ahead, redirect toward resolution, or shift the focus away from what carries weight. He follows. He allows return. He allows repetition. He remains present without requiring progress.

Re-engagement is not movement toward an outcome.

It is commitment to the process.

The second movement is using language that holds rather than directs. The listener's words should create space, not close it. Helpful language reflects what is present, acknowledges persistence, and allows multiple meanings:

"It makes sense that you would still be thinking about that."

"You're clear about why it happened, and it still seems to stay with you."

"That moment doesn't feel finished."

Unhelpful language resolves prematurely, narrows interpretation, and moves toward reassurance:

"You made the right call."

"You couldn't have done anything else."

"You need to let that go."

These statements may be true.

But they move the conversation away from what remains.

The third movement is recognizing conversational boundaries. Presence does not mean unlimited availability, and care does not mean removing all limits. The listener must remain clear about what the conversation is—and what it is not. This is not therapy. It is not confession. It is not problem-solving.

It is a space of recognition.

Boundaries protect both the speaker and the listener. They prevent the conversation from becoming a place where responsibility is transferred—where the listener becomes the one who must resolve what the speaker is carrying.

The listener does not take on the experience.

He stays with the person who is carrying it.

At the level of obligation, the listener is responsible for presence, not outcome. At the level of judgment, he does not evaluate the decision; he attends to the experience. At the level of agency, the speaker remains the one who moves, speaks, and understands.

The listener does not direct.

He accompanies.

The fourth movement is recognizing limits. Not every conversation can hold the full weight of moral injury, and not every listener is positioned to remain present in every situation. There are moments when additional support is needed—when the experience extends beyond what can be held in informal conversation, when patterns deepen into distress that requires structured care.

Recognizing this is not failure.

It is responsibility.

The listener may say:

"This feels like something that deserves more space than we have right now."

"I'm here with you, and I also think it could help to talk with someone who can stay with this more consistently."

This is not redirection away from care.

It is an extension of it.

The fifth movement is maintaining internal boundaries. The listener remains aware of his own responses—his impulse to fix, his discomfort with unresolved tension, his desire to reduce what is being carried. These responses are natural.

But they must be recognized.

The listener does not eliminate them.

He does not act on them.

He notices them.

And returns to presence.

This is the discipline of care.

The final movement is allowing the conversation to remain incomplete. The goal is not resolution, closure, or even relief.

It is recognition.

The conversation may end without a clear conclusion. The experience may still be present. The weight may not have shifted.

And yet, something has changed.

What was carried alone has been spoken. What was unarticulated has been recognized. What remained without language now has form.

This is enough.

Not because it resolves the experience.

But because it allows it to be held without distortion.

REFLECTION

When someone speaks about something that has not settled, what do you notice first?

The details of the story?

Or the weight that remains beneath it?

How quickly do you begin to respond?

What draws you toward speaking?

Is it the desire to help?

Or the discomfort of hearing what cannot be resolved?

When you listen, where does your attention move?

Toward explanation?

Toward outcome?

Or toward what continues to return?

What happens inside you when the conversation does not move forward?

When it circles?

When it lingers?

Do you interpret that as something to correct?

Or something to follow?

How do you recognize the difference between presence and participation?

At what point do you begin to carry what is not yours?

Can you feel that shift when it happens?

What helps you return?

When you leave a conversation, what remains with you?

What is yours to hold?

What must be released?

How do you practice that release?

Not as dismissal—

But as distinction?

When you speak, what does your language do?

Does it open space?

Or close it?

Does it allow what remains to stay visible?

Or does it move the conversation toward resolution too quickly?

What are you trying to protect?

The speaker?

Or yourself?

What would it mean to remain present without needing the conversation to end differently than it does?

To trust that recognition is enough?

To trust that being with someone in what remains is not incomplete care—

But faithful care?

What would it require of you to do this work over time?

Not once.

Not occasionally.

But consistently?

Where do you need boundaries?

Where do you need awareness?

Where do you need to return, again and again, to the discipline of presence?

And when you consider the people you serve, the roles you carry, the decisions you make—

Where might you also be the one who carries something that has not settled?

Who sits with you?

Who remains?

Who allows what you carry to be seen?

WHAT'S NEXT

You have seen how presence takes shape in relationship.

Next, we will turn toward repair and integration—not as resolution, but as a way of living with what remains.

Chapter 16

Repair and Integration

PART 1—LIVING WITH WHAT REMAINS

It does not end.

Not in the way we expect.

There is no single moment when what has been carried is set down, no clear point at which the experience resolves into something finished, something that can be left behind. The work continues, but not in the same way. There is a shift—not in what has happened, but in how it is held.

The one who carries has already moved through recognition. What was once diffuse has been named. What was once dismissed has been acknowledged. What was once carried without language now has form.

And still, it remains.

This is the beginning of repair—not the removal of what has been carried, but the reorientation of the one who carries it. Repair does not undo.

It reorganizes.

At first, this reorganization is subtle. The experience is no longer avoided, but it is not yet integrated. It is present, but it has not yet found its place. It appears at certain moments and recedes at others. It is no longer unrecognized, but it is not yet understood in relation to the whole of one's life.

This is where many assume something has gone wrong, because the expectation is resolution—the assumption that once something is named, it should diminish, settle, or disappear. But moral injury does not follow that pattern. Recognition does not remove persistence.

It clarifies it.

And clarity changes the nature of the work.

The question is no longer why this is still here.

The question becomes how to live with what remains.

This is not a question of endurance alone.

It is a question of identity.

What remains does not exist outside the person. It becomes part of how the person understands themselves, their decisions, their responsibilities, and their role. This is where the work deepens—not into resolution, but into integration.

At the level of experience, what once appeared as interruption begins to take on continuity. The experience no longer arrives only as disruption. It becomes something that can be anticipated, recognized, and held without the same degree of disorientation.

This does not mean it is easier.

It means it is known.

And what is known can be carried differently.

At the level of meaning, reconstruction begins. The initial interpretations—necessary, justified, unavoidable—remain, but they are no longer sufficient on their own. They expand to include what followed, what continues, what has been carried. Meaning is no longer singular.

It becomes layered.

The decision was necessary.

And it carried something that remains.

The action was justified.

And it did not end the experience.

Integration does not require choosing between these.

It requires holding both.

At the level of obligation, responsibility shifts. It is no longer only about what was required at the moment of decision. It extends into how the experience is now lived with, how it informs future action, and how it shapes attention and awareness. Responsibility becomes ongoing—not as burden, but as orientation.

At the level of judgment, evaluation softens. The question of right and wrong does not disappear, but it is no longer central. What becomes more central is how the experience has been incorporated—how it continues to influence perception, response, and understanding.

Judgment gives way to reflection.

At the level of agency, action continues—but it is altered. The one who carries does not return to the same way of acting. There is greater deliberation, greater awareness of consequence, and greater recognition of what decisions may carry beyond the moment in which they are made.

This is not hesitation.

It is integration.

At the level of legacy, the experience begins to take its place within a larger narrative. It is no longer an isolated moment that disrupts the story.

It becomes part of it.

Not as the defining feature.

But as a shaping one.

This is where repair becomes visible—not in the disappearance of the experience, but in its placement. It is no longer everywhere.

It is somewhere.

And that distinction matters, because what is everywhere overwhelms, while what is somewhere can be carried.

This movement is not linear. There are returns—moments when the experience feels as immediate as it once did, when the weight increases, when the sense of persistence intensifies, when the question returns with force.

This does not mean integration has failed.

It means the work continues.

Repair is not a state that is reached.

It is a practice that is maintained.

This is where the one who carries develops new forms of attention. He notices when the experience resurfaces, when it moves from background to foreground, when it begins to shape perception in ways that are not immediately visible. He does not suppress it. He does not give it full control.

He recognizes it.

And in recognizing it, he places it again—not by force, but by awareness.

This is the discipline of integration—not the elimination of what remains, but the ongoing work of holding it in relation to everything else.

Over time, something else begins to emerge—not resolution, but stability. The experience does not disappear, but it no longer destabilizes in the same way. It becomes part of how the person understands the world, part of how they approach decisions, and part of how they recognize weight in others.

It becomes instructive—not because it was desired, but because it was carried.

This is where the work of care and the work of integration intersect. The one who has been accompanied becomes capable of accompanying others—not because the experience has been resolved, but because it has been recognized and integrated. He does not speak from distance.

He speaks from proximity.

He knows what it is to carry something that remains, and he knows what it is to live with it.

This does not make the work easier.

But it makes it possible.

Repair does not restore the person to who they were before.

It allows them to continue as who they are now—changed, not diminished, carrying something that remains and still able to live.

PART 2—RECONSTRUCTION OF MEANING AND IDENTITY

What remains does not stay contained within the moment in which it was formed.

It extends—into interpretation, perception, and identity. This is where the work of integration deepens—not into resolution, but into reconstruction. Moral injury does not only affect what a person carries; it reshapes how a person understands themselves as the one who carries it. The disruption is not limited to the event.

It reaches into meaning.

At first, this disruption is difficult to locate. The individual may still describe the decision with clarity. The reasoning remains intact. The justification still holds.

But something underneath has shifted.

The question is no longer only about what happened.

It becomes what this says about the person who carries it.

This question is not always spoken.

But it persists.

At the level of meaning, the initial interpretations—necessary, justified, unavoidable—begin to feel incomplete. They explain the decision, but they do not fully account for the experience. There is a gap between what is understood and what is carried, and this gap is where reconstruction begins, because meaning can no longer remain singular.

It must expand.

The decision was necessary.

And it left something unresolved.

The action was justified.

And it altered how the individual understands what they are capable of.

The outcome was unavoidable.

And it changed how the world is perceived.

These are not contradictions.

They are layers.

Reconstruction requires holding them together without collapsing them into one.

At the level of identity, this becomes more complex. Before the experience, identity often includes a sense of coherence—a belief that values, actions, and understanding align in a stable way. Decisions may be difficult, but they fit within an existing framework. Moral injury disrupts that coherence—not by eliminating values, but by revealing their limits.

The individual begins to see that it is possible to act in alignment with responsibility and still carry something that does not resolve, to make a necessary decision and still experience it as costly in ways that cannot be reduced to outcome or intention.

This realization does not destroy identity.

But it changes it.

The person can no longer understand themselves in the same way, and this creates a new question—who they are now, knowing what they have done and what they carry. This question cannot be answered quickly or resolved through explanation.

It requires time and attention.

At the level of experience, reconstruction begins as reorientation. Assumptions that once held no longer do. The world appears more complex, more layered, less predictable. Decisions are no longer understood only in terms of right and wrong, but in terms of consequence, persistence, and impact.

This is not confusion.

It is expansion.

At the level of meaning, the individual begins to integrate the experience into a broader framework. This does not remove its tension. It allows the experience to exist within a larger understanding of life, responsibility, and limitation. Meaning becomes less about resolution and more about coherence—not coherence as simplicity, but coherence as inclusion.

Nothing is excluded.

The experience is not set aside.

It is placed within.

At the level of obligation, identity begins to include what has been carried. Responsibility is no longer understood only as action in the moment, but as awareness over time. The individual becomes more attentive to what decisions may carry, more aware of limits, and more conscious of the cost of participation.

This does not lead to withdrawal.

It leads to depth.

At the level of judgment, self-evaluation shifts. The question is no longer whether one is good or bad, right or wrong, justified or mistaken. Those categories remain, but they are no longer sufficient. Evaluation becomes centered on how the individual holds what they have carried—whether it is acknowledged, whether it informs, whether it is avoided or engaged.

Judgment becomes reflective—less about verdict, more about orientation.

At the level of agency, identity is expressed through action. The individual continues to decide, engage, and participate—but not in the same way. There is greater awareness of consequence, greater attentiveness to impact, and greater recognition of complexity.

This is not paralysis.

It is formation.

The person is not less capable.

They are differently aware.

At the level of legacy, the experience becomes part of the story the individual tells about themselves. It is no longer an isolated disruption.

It is incorporated.

Not as the defining moment.

But as a formative one.

The story changes—not in its facts, but in its meaning.

This is where reconstruction becomes visible—not in a single realization, but in an ongoing process of integration. The individual revisits the experience, not to resolve it, but to understand how it fits within the whole of who they are becoming.

This process is not linear. There are returns—moments when old questions resurface, when disruption intensifies, when identity feels unsettled again.

This does not mean reconstruction has failed.

It means it is still unfolding.

Reconstruction is not a single act.

It is a sustained practice.

Over time, something stabilizes—not because the questions disappear, but because the individual learns how to live with them. The tension between what was necessary and what remains does not dissolve.

It is incorporated.

The person no longer needs to resolve it in order to continue.

They carry it.

And in carrying it, they are changed—not broken, not diminished, but expanded. Their understanding of themselves is no longer limited to what they intended, believed, or hoped. It includes what they have done, what they have experienced, and what they continue to carry.

This is the reconstruction of identity—not a return to what was, but the formation of something that can hold more than what was possible before.

And this formation does not end.

It continues as long as the work continues, as long as decisions are made, as long as responsibility is carried.

The question is not whether identity will change.

It is how that change will be held.

PART 3—MOVEMENT TOWARD INTEGRATION

He did not notice the change all at once.

There was no moment when the experience shifted from unresolved to integrated, no clear transition from carrying to having carried. The experience still returned—the same moment, the same decision, the same sense of something that had not settled—but something in how it was encountered had begun to change.

At first, the change appeared in small ways. When the memory surfaced, it did not immediately take over. There was still weight, still presence, still persistence—but there was also distance. Not separation, not avoidance, but space. He could see it and still remain where he was.

This was new. Before, the experience had been immediate. It drew him into itself without warning or choice. When it appeared, it was not something he observed.

It was something he was inside of.

Now there were moments when he could recognize it as it emerged—feel the shift, notice the movement of attention, the return of certain thoughts, the way the past entered the present. In that recognition, something else became possible.

He did not have to follow it completely.

He could stay.

This did not happen consistently. There were still times when the experience overtook him—when immediacy returned, when the weight felt as strong as before, when the question resurfaced with the same intensity.

These moments were not failures.

They were part of the process.

Integration does not eliminate return.

It changes how return is encountered.

Over time, he began to notice patterns—not only in the experience itself, but in how it moved through him. Certain situations brought it forward: particular decisions, certain conversations, moments of stillness. He began to anticipate these—not with fear, but with awareness. This anticipation did not prevent the experience from emerging, but it reduced its unpredictability.

And unpredictability had been part of what made it difficult.

The experience was no longer only something that happened to him.

It became something he recognized.

At the level of meaning, something similar was taking place. The initial interpretations had not changed. The decision was still necessary. The conditions were still what they had been. The outcome had not been altered.

But the way he held those interpretations had expanded.

He no longer needed them to resolve the experience.

He allowed them to exist alongside it.

The decision made sense.

And it still remained.

He no longer tried to reconcile these into a single conclusion.

He held them as they were.

This did not remove the tension.

But it made it livable.

At the level of identity, the change was more gradual. There had been a time when the experience felt like a contradiction—something that did not fit within how he understood himself. It had raised questions not only about what had happened, but about who he was in relation to it.

Those questions had not disappeared.

But they had shifted.

Instead of asking what the experience said about him, he began to ask how to live as the person who had experienced it. This shift did not answer the question.

It reframed it.

It moved it from evaluation to continuation.

At the level of action, this became visible in how he approached decisions. He did not withdraw from responsibility or avoid situations that carried weight, but he did not approach them in the same way. There was greater awareness, greater attention, and greater recognition of what might follow.

This did not make decisions easier.

But it made them more conscious.

He no longer assumed that a decision would end when it was made.

He understood that it might continue.

And this understanding changed how he entered into it.

At the level of relationship, something else began to emerge. He became more attentive to others—more aware of when someone was carrying something that had not settled, more capable of recognizing patterns of return, and more willing to remain in conversations that did not resolve.

This was not because he had mastered the experience.

It was because he had lived within it.

He recognized what it looked like, what it felt like, and what it required—not explanation, not resolution, but presence. This did not mean he always knew what to do.

It meant he knew how to remain.

Over time, the experience began to take its place. It did not disappear, but it was no longer everywhere. It appeared, remained, and then receded—not completely, but enough that it no longer defined every moment and could be carried alongside other parts of life—work, relationships, decisions.

Life continued.

And the experience continued within it.

This is what integration looks like—not the absence of what remains, but its placement. The experience no longer exists as interruption.

It exists as part of the structure.

This does not mean it is always visible.

But it is always present.

And that presence informs without overwhelming.

There are still moments when it returns with force—when persistence sharpens, when the weight increases, when the past feels immediate again. These moments are not signs that integration has been lost.

They are reminders that integration is ongoing.

He does not interpret them as failure.

He recognizes them as return.

And he responds as he has learned to respond—he notices, he allows, he places.

This is not resolution.

It is practice.

Over time, that practice becomes something like stability—not the stability of certainty, but the stability of knowing how to live with what is not resolved. He no longer asks when it will end.

He understands that it may not.

And this understanding does not diminish him.

It grounds him.

He continues—not because the experience has disappeared, but because he has learned how to carry it.

PART 4—PRACTICES FOR LONG-TERM REPAIR

Repair is not a single act.

It is not achieved through insight alone, nor completed through one moment of recognition or one period of reflection. What has been carried does not resolve because it has been understood.

It is lived with.

And because it is lived with, repair must take the form of practice—not practices that eliminate what remains, but practices that allow what remains to be carried without distortion.

The first practice is attention—not general awareness, but deliberate attention to how the experience moves over time. The one who carries begins to notice when the experience shifts from background to foreground—when something surfaces, when a memory returns, when a sense of weight increases without immediate cause.

This noticing is not passive.

It is intentional.

He learns to recognize early movements—the subtle changes in thought, the return of particular questions, the reappearance of specific moments. Attention does not prevent the experience, but it changes how it is encountered.

What is noticed is less likely to overwhelm.

The second practice is naming—not explaining, not resolving, but naming. When the experience surfaces, the individual gives it language—not to contain it, but to recognize it. This may be internal, or it may be spoken in the presence of another.

"This is that moment returning."

"This is what remains."

This language does not reduce the experience.

It places it.

Naming interrupts the tendency to reinterpret the experience as something else—as fatigue, distraction, or something to dismiss or push away.

It clarifies.

The third practice is placement. Once recognized and named, the experience must be situated—not removed, not suppressed, but placed within the broader context of the person's life. This is the work of integration: ensuring that what remains does not expand to fill everything, but is held alongside everything else.

He returns to what is present—to where he is, to what is required now. This is not avoidance.

It is orientation.

The experience is acknowledged.

And then placed.

The fourth practice is return. Because placement does not last indefinitely, the experience will surface again. When it does, the process repeats—not identically, but consistently: attention, naming, placement.

Over time, this repetition becomes familiar—not easier, but known.

Return is not regression.

It is continuation.

The fifth practice is shared recognition. What is carried alone remains heavier than what is carried in the presence of another. The individual learns not to isolate the experience entirely—not to speak about it constantly, but not to contain it completely. He identifies spaces where it can be acknowledged—conversations where presence is possible, where what remains can be spoken without being reduced.

This is not dependency.

It is relational integration.

The experience becomes part of how he relates to others—not as something that defines the interaction, but as something that can be present within it.

The sixth practice is boundary. The individual learns to recognize what is his to carry and what is not. This includes not only his own experience, but the experiences of others. As he becomes more capable of recognizing moral weight in others, there is a risk of taking on what does not belong to him.

Boundary is not withdrawal.

It is clarity.

He remains present.

But he does not absorb.

This practice protects the sustainability of repair. Without it, the work becomes cumulative in a way that cannot be maintained.

The seventh practice is re-engagement. Repair does not require withdrawal from responsibility. The individual continues to act, decide, and participate in roles that carry consequence—but with awareness. He does not return to unawareness or assume that decisions end when they are made.

He understands that they may continue.

And he enters them with that understanding.

This is not hesitation.

It is informed engagement.

The eighth practice is reflection over time—not immediate analysis, but periodic return to the experience in a way that allows it to be seen within a larger arc. The individual revisits what has been carried—not to resolve it, but to understand how it has changed, how it has been integrated, and how it continues to function within his life.

This reflection is not constant.

It is intentional.

It creates continuity.

The ninth practice is acceptance of incompletion. This may be the most difficult—the recognition that the experience may not resolve, that the sense of persistence may not disappear, that the questions may not be fully answered.

Acceptance does not mean approval.

It means recognition.

The work is not to eliminate what remains.

It is to live with it.

The final practice is continuation. The individual does not wait for the experience to resolve before moving forward. He continues to live, engage, and participate—not in spite of what remains, but with it.

This is the culmination of repair—not the restoration of what was, but the ability to continue as who one has become.

These practices are not steps.

They do not move in sequence.

They recur.

They overlap.

They return.

Over time, they form something less like a method
and more like a way of living.

Reflection

What remains for you?

Not what has been explained.

Not what has been resolved.

What remains?

When you think about the moments you have carried—the decisions, the outcomes, the experiences that did not settle—how do they live within you now?

Do they interrupt?
Or have they found a place?
What has changed—not in what happened, but in how you hold it?
When something returns, how do you meet it?
Do you resist it?
Follow it?
Or recognize it?
Can you feel the difference between being inside the experience
and being able to see it?
What allows that shift?
How has what you carry shaped how you understand yourself?
Not who you were before—
but who you are now?
What questions has it left you with?
Are you trying to answer them?
Or are you learning how to live with them?
What does it mean, for you, to hold more than one truth at the same time?
That something was necessary—
and that it still remains?
Where do you feel tension?
Do you try to resolve it?
Or can you allow it to be part of your understanding?
What has become more visible to you because of what you have carried?
About decisions?
About responsibility?
About the limits of control?
How has it changed the way you see others?
Can you recognize when someone else is carrying something that has not settled?
How do you respond?
Do you move toward explanation?
Or toward presence?
What practices help you remain steady?
What helps you notice?
Name?
Place?

Return?
Who do you allow to share in what you carry?
Who remains with you without trying to resolve you?
What boundaries sustain you?
What protects your ability to continue?
Where do you still feel the need for resolution?
What would it mean to release that expectation?
Not because the experience no longer matters—
but because it does?
What would it mean to live without needing it to end?
What would it mean to trust that continuation is not failure—
but formation?
And as you consider the life you are living now—
the decisions you are making,
the responsibilities you are carrying,
the people you are with—
how is what remains shaping the way you move forward?
Not as interruption.
But as part of the structure.
Not as something to be removed.
But as something that has been carried
and continues to inform who you are becoming.

WHAT'S NEXT

We have seen that integration is ongoing, not complete.

Next, we move into the conclusion—where all of this is gathered into a way of continuing with what remains.

Conclusion

Living With What Remains

PART 1—THE WEIGHT THAT DOES NOT DISAPPEAR

IT DOES NOT LEAVE.

Not completely.

There is no final moment when what has been carried disappears, no point at which the weight resolves into something that no longer needs to be held. Even after recognition, after care, after the long work of integration, something remains—not as it was, but not gone.

This is often the quiet surprise at the end of the process: the realization that the goal was never removal.

It was relationship.

What has been carried does not vanish. It changes, and the one who carries it changes with it.

The expectation of resolution runs deep. It shapes how we approach difficulty, how we understand healing, and how we imagine the end of disruption. We assume that understanding will bring closure, that naming will bring release, that time will create distance.

Sometimes it does.

But not always.

Moral injury does not follow that pattern. It does not resolve because it is understood.

It remains.

And this is not failure.

It is reality.

The weight that does not disappear is not evidence that something has gone wrong in the process of repair. It is evidence of what the experience was. Some experiences do not conclude.

They continue.

And the work is not to force them to end, but to learn how to live with them as they are.

At first, this can feel like something unfinished—something that should have been resolved but was not. The mind returns to it, searching for closure, trying to bring it to an end.

Over time, a different understanding takes shape.

The experience is not unfinished.

It is ongoing.

This distinction changes everything. An unfinished experience demands resolution, while an ongoing experience requires integration. The shift is not from carrying to no longer carrying, but from carrying without orientation to carrying with awareness.

The weight remains, but it no longer exists without context. It has been seen, named, and placed—brought into relation with the rest of one's life.

This does not make it lighter in every moment.

But it makes it livable.

The one who carries begins to recognize that the goal was never to remove the weight, but to learn how to hold it without distortion. What once overwhelmed can now be approached. What once interrupted everything can now exist alongside other things.

This is not resolution.

It is integration.

Integration does not diminish the significance of what has been carried.

It honors it—by allowing it to remain without requiring it to disappear.

At the level of experience, the weight is still present. It returns, makes itself known, and carries a sense of persistence—but it is no longer the only thing present. It shares space with work, with relationships, with moments of clarity, with moments of rest.

This sharing of space is not accidental.

It is the result of practice.

The one who carries has learned how to place the experience—not to remove it, but to situate it. They recognize when it surfaces, name it without reducing it, and allow it to exist without letting it expand into everything.

This is a learned way of living.

Not a solution.

A practice.

At the level of meaning, the experience continues to hold its complexity. It does not simplify into a single interpretation. It remains layered—necessary and costly, justified and unresolved, understood and still present.

This layering does not weaken meaning.

It deepens it, allowing the experience to be held in its fullness—not reduced, not explained away, but included.

At the level of identity, the weight becomes part of how the individual understands themselves—not as a defining failure or something that negates who they are, but as something that has shaped them. The person who carries is not the same as the person who came before.

But they are not less.

They are more aware, more attentive, and more capable of recognizing what others may not see.

This is not a reward for suffering.

It is a consequence of carrying—and it comes with responsibility: to live in a way that acknowledges what has been learned without being defined entirely by what has been experienced.

At the level of action, life continues. Decisions are still made. Responsibilities are still carried. Participation does not end because the experience remains.

But participation changes.

There is greater awareness of consequence, greater recognition of what decisions may carry beyond the moment in which they are made, and greater attentiveness to what cannot be controlled.

This does not make action easier.

But it makes it more grounded.

At the level of relationship, something else becomes possible. The one who has learned to live with what remains becomes capable of recognizing it in others—not through analysis, but through familiarity. They know what it looks like when something has not settled, what it feels like when something continues, and what is required.

Not explanation.

Not resolution.

Presence.

This is where the work extends beyond the individual. What has been carried becomes part of how one remains with others—not because it has been resolved, but because it has been integrated.

This is the quiet transformation at the center of this work.

The weight does not disappear, but it becomes part of how one lives—not as interruption, but as structure; not as something to be removed, but as something tobe held.

And this holding is not static.

It changes over time.

There are still returns—moments when the weight feels closer, sharper, more immediate. These moments do not undo the work.

They are part of it.

The one who carries does not interpret them as failure.

They recognize them as continuation.

And they respond as they have learned to respond—through attention, through naming, through placement.

Through practice.

This is what it means to live with what remains: not to solve it, not to end it, but to carry it in a way that allows life to continue—not despite it, but with it.

PART 2—INTEGRATION OVER RESOLUTION

For much of our lives, we are taught to move toward resolution. Problems are solved. Conflicts are settled. Questions are answered. Difficulty is approached with the expectation that it can be worked through, understood, and brought to a point of completion.

This expectation shapes how we understand healing, how we measure progress, and what we believe it means for something to be "over." When something does not resolve—when it continues, when it returns, when it remains—we assume that something has gone wrong, either in the experience or in ourselves.

This is the framework most people bring to moral injury: that if it were properly understood, it would diminish; that if it were properly processed, it would resolve; that if enough time passes, it would disappear.

But moral injury does not follow this pattern. It does not resolve because it has been understood, disappear because it has been named, or conclude because time has passed.

It remains.

And because it remains, the framework must change.

The work is not resolution.

It is integration.

This shift is rarely immediate. It often begins with resistance—the recognition that what has been carried is not diminishing in the way one expected. The individual may continue to search for a way to bring the experience to a close, to find the explanation that will finally settle it, to reach the point where it no longer returns.

This search is understandable.

It is also limited.

Because it assumes that the experience is incomplete.

But what if it is not incomplete?

What if it is ongoing?

This question changes the orientation of the work. An incomplete experience demands resolution, while an ongoing experience requires integration. Integration does not seek to end what remains; it seeks to place it—bringing it into relation with the rest of one's life in a way that allows it to exist without dominating everything else.

This is not passive.

It is active, deliberate, and sustained.

At the level of experience, integration means learning to recognize what remains without being overtaken by it. The experience still surfaces, still carries weight, still has presence—but it is no longer the only thing present. It is held alongside other realities.

At the level of meaning, integration means allowing complexity to remain. The experience is not simplified into a single interpretation but held in its layered form—necessary and costly, justified and unresolved, understood and still present.

This complexity is not a problem to be solved.

It is a reality to be held.

At the level of identity, integration means incorporating what has been carried into how one understands oneself. The individual does not return to who they were before.

They become someone capable of holding more—more awareness, more complexity, more responsibility.

This is not a loss of identity.

It is its expansion.

At the level of action, integration means continuing to engage with life while carrying what remains. Decisions are still made. Responsibilities are still assumed. Participation does not end.

But it is no longer unexamined.

The individual acts with the awareness that what is done may continue beyond the moment in which it is done. This awareness does not prevent action.

It deepens it.

At the level of relationship, integration allows the individual to remain with others in a different way. The one who has learned to live with what remains becomes capable of recognizing it in others—not through analysis, but through familiarity. They know what persistence feels like, what unresolved experience looks like, and what is required.

Not explanation.

Not resolution.

Presence.

Integration does not remove the weight.

It changes the relationship to it.

The individual no longer asks how to get rid of what remains.

They ask how to live with it.

This question does not have a single answer. It unfolds over time—shaped by experience, refined through practice, and revisited through return.

This is why integration cannot be reduced to a technique. It is not something that can be applied once and completed.

It is a way of living.

And like any way of living, it requires ongoing attention.

There are still moments when the pull toward resolution returns—when the individual wishes for the experience to end, for the weight to lift, for the persistence to stop. These moments are not mistakes.

They are part of the tension.

Because the desire for resolution does not disappear simply because integration has begun.

It remains.

And it must be held as well.

This is part of the work—to hold both the desire for resolution and the reality of what remains, not as opposing forces, but as part of the same experience.

Over time, something shifts—not in the presence of the experience, but in the expectations placed upon it. The individual no longer requires the experience to end in order to continue and no longer interprets its persistence as failure.

They recognize it as part of what it is.

And this recognition brings a different kind of stability—not the stability of resolution, but the stability of orientation.

They know how to meet what returns.

They know how to place what remains.

They know how to continue.

This is integration—not the end of what has been carried, but the beginning of living with it.

PART 3—ONGOING MORAL LIFE AFTER INJURY

There is no clear line between before and after.

No point at which the experience is finished and life resumes in its previous form. Life does not pause long enough for that kind of transition. It continues—while the experience is still present, while the weight is still carried, while the questions remain.

This is what makes the return to ordinary life feel unfamiliar.

Nothing has stopped.

And yet, everything has changed.

The individual returns to the same roles—work, responsibility, relationships, decision-making. The structure of life remains recognizable, but the way it is inhabited is different. What was once assumed is now considered. What was once automatic is now examined. What was once invisible is now seen.

This is not disruption.

It is awareness.

At first, this awareness can feel like a burden. Decisions take longer. The weight of consequence is more visible. The sense of what may continue beyond the moment of action is more present. It can feel as though something has been lost—a kind of simplicity, a kind of ease.

Over time, however, something else becomes clear.

What has been lost is not capacity.

It is unawareness.

And what has been gained is not hesitation.

It is depth.

The individual continues to act—not less, but differently. There is greater attention to what decisions may carry, greater recognition that responsibility does not end with action, and greater awareness that some outcomes cannot be controlled and some consequences cannot be prevented.

This does not lead to withdrawal.

It leads to a different form of engagement—less certain, but more grounded.

At the level of daily life, this shift is often quiet. It does not announce itself in dramatic ways. It appears in small adjustments—in the pause before a decision, in the recognition of weight in a conversation, and in the willingness to remain with something that does not resolve.

The individual does not become someone else.

They become more fully aware of who they are within what they carry.

At the level of relationship, this awareness changes how others are encountered. The one who has lived with what remains begins to recognize it in others—not through explicit disclosure, but through tone, repetition, and what lingers in the space between what is said and what is not. They notice when something has not settled and when a conversation is not moving forward—not because it lacks clarity, but because something within it remains unresolved.

And they know what to do.

Not because they have learned a method.

But because they have lived the experience.

They remain.

This is one of the quiet continuations of moral injury—the way it shapes how one is able to be present to others. What has been carried becomes part of how one recognizes, listens, and stays.

This is not a role.

It is a way of being.

At the level of decision-making, the individual no longer assumes that clarity will eliminate cost. There is a deeper awareness that even necessary decisions may carry something forward, that justification does not prevent persistence, and that responsibility extends beyond the moment in which action is taken.

This awareness does not prevent decision.

But it removes the illusion that decision ends the matter.

The individual acts with the knowledge that something may remain, and this knowledge changes how they enter into action—not with certainty, but with attentiveness.

At the level of internal life, the experience continues to move. There are still returns—moments when something surfaces without warning, when the past feels immediate, when the sense of persistence sharpens.

These moments do not disappear.

They are part of what it means to carry.

But they are no longer disorienting in the same way.

The individual recognizes them, names them, places them, and continues. This rhythm—recognition, naming, placement, continuation—becomes part of daily life. Not always consciously and not always perfectly, but consistently enough that the experience no longer overwhelms in the same way.

This is not resolution.

It is familiarity.

And familiarity changes how something is carried.

At the level of identity, the individual no longer seeks to return to who they were before. That version of self is not recoverable—not because it has been destroyed, but because it has been expanded. The person now includes what they have carried, what they have done, what they have experienced, and what remains.

This inclusion does not simplify identity.

It deepens it.

They are not defined by the experience.

But they are shaped by it.

And this shaping is ongoing.

At the level of time, something else becomes visible. The experience does not fade in a straight line or diminish steadily.

It moves.

There are periods when it feels distant and periods when it feels close, moments when it feels settled and moments when it does not. This variability is not a sign of instability.

It is a characteristic of what continues.

The individual no longer measures progress by absence. They recognize movement, placement, and the ability to continue.

And this becomes its own form of stability—not the stability of certainty, but the stability of knowing how to live within what is not resolved.

At the level of vocation—whether named as such or not—the experience begins to inform how the individual understands their place in the world. Not in a grand or abstract way, but in a grounded and specific way. They know what weight looks like, what persistence feels like, and what it means to carry something that does not disappear.

And this knowledge shapes how they move, how they speak, and how they remain.

This is not transformation into something new.

It is continuation with awareness.

The life that follows moral injury is not a different life.

It is the same life, lived differently—not because the past has been resolved, but because it has been integrated.

The individual does not leave the experience behind.

They bring it with them.

Not as something that interrupts.

But as something that informs.

And in that movement, something becomes possible—not the end of what remains, but the ability to live fully within it.

PART 4—CONTINUATION

There is no final step.

No point at which the work is complete, no moment when what has been carried is fully resolved and set aside. What remains does not end. It changes—and the one who carries it changes with it.

The work, then, is not to reach an ending.

It is to continue—not aimlessly and not without direction, but with an orientation shaped by what has been seen, named, and integrated.

This orientation is not complicated.

But it is not easy.

It is sustained through practice—through the repeated movements of noticing what is present, naming what is returning, and placing what has surfaced within the context of a life that continues. These are not steps to be completed but patterns to be lived. They do not unfold in sequence; they recur, overlap, and return.

At times, the work will feel steady. The experience will be recognizable, the weight manageable, the movement familiar.

At other times, it will not.

There will be moments when what remains feels closer, sharper, more immediate—when persistence intensifies and the desire for resolution returns with force.

These moments do not undo the work.

They are part of it.

The task is not to prevent their return, but to meet them as they are—with attention, clarity, and the practices that have been learned. This is what sustains the work over time: not the absence of difficulty, but the presence of orientation.

The one who carries does not need to resolve what remains in order to live.

They need to know how to carry it.

And this knowledge is not theoretical.

It is lived—formed through repetition, through return, through the ongoing act of placing what has surfaced back into relation with everything else.

Over time, this becomes something like stability—not the stability of certainty, but the stability of familiarity. The individual knows what it means when something returns, how to meet it, and how to continue.

This is enough.

Not because it answers every question, but because it allows life to go on without requiring those questions to be answered first.

The desire for resolution may remain—the hope that something will settle, that the weight will lessen, that persistence will fade.

This, too, is part of what is carried.

And it, too, must be held—not resisted or indulged, but recognized, placed, and allowed.

This is the quiet discipline at the center of this work: to hold what remains without requiring it to end, to continue without waiting for completion, and to live within what has been carried.

This is not resignation.

It is not giving up.

It is a form of fidelity—to reality, to experience, to the truth of what has been carried and what continues.

Within that fidelity, something else becomes possible—not resolution, but a life that is not defined by the need for it.

The individual does not move beyond what has been carried.

They move with it.

And in that movement, they remain capable of action, of relationship, and of presence.

They remain capable of living.

This is where the work comes to rest—not in conclusion, but in continuation; not in the absence of what remains, but in the ability to live with it.

You do not need it to end
in order to continue.

REFLECTION

What remains for you now?

Not what you have understood.

Not what you have named.

What remains?

When you think about the moments you carry—the decisions, the outcomes, the experiences that did not settle—how do they live within you now?

Do they still interrupt?

Or have they begun to find a place?

When something returns, how do you meet it?

Do you resist it?

Follow it?

Or recognize it?

Can you feel the difference between being inside the experience
and being able to see it?

What has allowed that shift?

What has changed—not in what happened,
but in how you hold it?

What does it mean, for you, to carry something that does not end?

Do you still expect it to resolve?

Or are you beginning to understand it as something ongoing?

What happens when you stop asking when it will be over
and begin asking how to live with it as it is?

What becomes possible then?

How has what you carry shaped how you understand yourself?

Not who you were before—
but who you are now?

What have you learned about responsibility?

About consequence?

About the limits of control?

How has it changed the way you move through the world?
How you make decisions?
How you remain with others?
Can you recognize when someone else is carrying something that has not settled?
How do you respond?
Do you move toward explanation?
Or toward presence?
Who remains with you in what you carry?
Who allows what remains to be present
without trying to resolve it?
What practices have you learned?
What helps you notice?
Name?
Place?
Continue?
Where do you still feel the pull toward resolution?
What would it mean to hold that desire
without letting it determine what comes next?
What would it mean to trust that continuation is not failure—
but formation?
And as you consider the life you are living now—
the responsibilities you carry,
the relationships you are part of,
the decisions still ahead—
how is what remains shaping the way you move forward?
Not as interruption.
But as part of the structure.
Not as something to be removed.
But as something that has been carried
and continues to inform who you are becoming.

FINAL INVITATION

You do not need to resolve what remains.
You need to know how to live with it.
And you are already learning how.

Appendix

Moral Injury Tools

HOW TO USE THIS APPENDIX

THESE TOOLS ARE NOT designed to diagnose, fix, or resolve moral injury.

They are designed to help you:

- Recognize what is happening
- Name what is being carried
- Remain present with yourself or another
- Support integration over time

They are not steps.

They are supports.

Use them flexibly, return to them often, and adapt them to your context.

TOOL 1—MIR FRAMEWORK (MORAL INJURY RECOGNITION)

Use this when you suspect moral injury may be present.

M—Moral Tension

- "Something about this doesn't sit right."
- Conflict between values and actions (yours or others')

I—Impact That Persists

- The experience continues beyond the event
- Replays, intrusive thoughts, emotional return

R—Rupture in Meaning or Identity

- "I don't see myself the same way anymore"
- Loss of coherence in worldview or self-understanding

—

Quick Field Questions

- What feels unresolved here?
- What keeps returning?
- What feels different about how you see yourself or the world?

TOOL 2—M.O.R.A.L. ASSESSMENT

A deeper lens for understanding what is being carried.

M—Meaning

- What does this experience mean to you now?
- Has that meaning changed over time?

O—Obligation

- What responsibility do you feel you carry?
- Is it defined, or does it feel open-ended?

R—Relationship

- Who else is connected to this experience?
- Has it changed how you relate to others?

A—Action

- What decisions were made?
- What continues because of those decisions?

L—Legacy

- How is this experience still shaping you?
- What has it become part of?

—

Use

- Personal reflection
- Guided conversation
- Debrief after difficult events

TOOL 3—PRESENCE-BASED CONVERSATION GUIDE

For sitting with someone in moral pain.

Opening

- "Do you want to talk about what's been staying with you?"
- "What has been hard to put down?"

Exploring

- "What part of this feels unresolved?"
- "What keeps coming back to you?"
- "How has this affected how you see yourself?"

Holding (not fixing)

- "That makes sense."
- "I can hear how much this still matters."
- "You don't have to resolve this right now."

Closing

- "What helps you carry this when it comes back?"
- "Who else knows you're carrying this?"

—

Avoid

- Explaining it away
- Reframing too quickly
- Offering premature reassurance

TOOL 4—BOUNDARY CHECK

For caregivers, responders, and clergy.

Ask Yourself

- What is mine to carry?
- What belongs to the other person?
- Am I taking on weight that is not mine?

Indicators You Are Over-Carrying

- Emotional exhaustion tied to others' experiences
- Difficulty separating your role from their story
- Persistent internalization of others' pain

Reorientation

- "I can remain present without absorbing."
- "My role is to accompany, not carry for them."

TOOL 5—THE PRACTICE LOOP

A simple integration rhythm.

1. Notice
    - Something is returning
2. Name
    - "This is that moment"
    - "This is what remains"
3. Place
    - Bring attention back to the present
    - Situate the experience within your life
4. Continue
    - Return to what is in front of you

—

Important

- This is not a one-time process
- It repeats over time
- Familiarity—not resolution—is the goal

TOOL 6—INDICATORS OF INTEGRATION

Signs that integration (not resolution) is occurring:

- The experience still returns—but does not overwhelm every time
- You can recognize it as it emerges
- You can speak about it without reducing it
- It exists alongside other parts of life
- It informs you without defining everything

TOOL 7—REFLECTION PROMPTS (ONGOING USE)

Use periodically—not constantly.

- What has shifted in how I carry this?
- What feels different about how it returns?
- What helps me remain when it surfaces?
- What am I learning about living with it?

WHEN ADDITIONAL SUPPORT IS NEEDED

These tools are not a substitute for professional care.

Consider additional support if:

- The experience becomes overwhelming or unmanageable
- Daily functioning is significantly impaired
- There is persistent despair, isolation, or loss of meaning
- You are unable to remain present with the experience at all

Seeking support is not failure.
It is continuation.

FINAL NOTE

These tools will not remove what remains.
They will help you carry it.
Return to them.
Use them in the field.
Use them in quiet moments.
Use them with others.
Over time, they will become less like tools
and more like a way of living.

Acknowledgements

THIS BOOK WAS NOT written alone.

It may have been shaped in quiet rooms, in long stretches of reflection, and in the discipline of putting words to what often resists language—but it was formed in the presence of others.

To those who have carried what remains and allowed me to witness it—thank you. Your honesty, your restraint, your willingness to speak without resolution shaped more of these pages than you may realize. Much of what is written here was learned not from theory, but from sitting with you.

To those who serve in moments that do not resolve—disaster responders, clergy, caregivers, and all who remain present when others cannot—this work is, in many ways, yours. You taught me that presence matters more than explanation, and that staying is often the most difficult and most necessary form of care.

To my colleagues and companions in this work, especially within disaster spiritual care and the broader community of those attending to moral injury, thank you for your insight, your questions, and your commitment to doing this work with integrity. You have sharpened my thinking and steadied my practice.

To those who have walked alongside me personally—family, friends, and those who have made space for the long and sometimes quiet work of writing—thank you for your patience and your presence. You have held more than you were asked to hold, and you have done so with grace.

To the communities that have shaped my vocation—including the church, and particularly those within the Presbyterian Church (U.S.A.)—thank you for forming in me a way of attending to human experience that takes both faith and complexity seriously.

To those who read early drafts, asked hard questions, and resisted easy answers—your influence is present on every page. This book is better because you did not allow it to become simpler than the reality it seeks to describe.

And finally, to those who will read this book while carrying something that does not resolve—this was written with you in mind. Not to explain what you carry, and not to take it from you, but to accompany you as you continue.

You are not alone in carrying what remains.

About the Author

Rev. Gregory C. Smith, PhD, is a retired Minister of Word and Sacrament in the Presbyterian Church (U.S.A.), where he served congregations for over thirty years. His work has consistently focused on the intersection of faith, human experience, and the realities that do not resolve neatly—especially in times of crisis, loss, and moral complexity.

Dr. Smith has been deeply engaged in disaster response and spiritual care, including service as a board member of the Iowa Disaster Human Resources Council. His work alongside disaster responders, caregivers, and faith-based organizations has shaped his understanding of moral injury as a lived and ongoing experience rather than a problem to be solved.

He is the author of numerous books exploring moral injury, public life, and spiritual care, including works published by Wipf and Stock. Across both his nonfiction and fiction writing, his focus remains consistent: to attend carefully to what people carry, especially when it does not resolve, and to offer language and frameworks that support presence, integrity, and continuation.

Dr. Smith writes not to provide easy answers, but to accompany readers as they navigate complex and enduring human experiences. His work is grounded in the conviction that meaning is not always found in resolution, but often in how we learn to live with what remains.